Susan had seemed much the same as she showed up for questioning that day. Dressed in jeans and hooded sweatshirt, she hadn't appeared particularly agitated when the sheriff arranged to have her picked up at the Russell home that afternoon. But something within her had clearly changed.

Within two hours Susan Smith began to tell Sheriff Howard Wells what happened on the night of October 25.

Susan Smith talked about the crushing isolation she had felt as she had driven her Mazda along the dark highway, consumed by the desire to end her life. She had left home that evening planning to drive around for a while and then take the boys to her mother's house.

In her confession, Susan Smith maintained that she pulled off Highway 49 onto the dark, winding road that led to John D. Long Lake because she was ready to die. As for her children, Susan said that she believed they would be better off with her, with God, than left motherless and alone.

In her plan, it would be the three of them—Susan, Michael, and Alex. They would die together . . . .

St. Martin's Paperbacks Titles
by Maria Eftimiades

LETHAL LOLITA
"MY NAME IS KATHERINE"
GARDEN OF GRAVES
SINS OF THE MOTHER

SINS
of the
MOTHER

MARIA EFTIMIADES

ST. MARTIN'S PAPERBACKS

SINS OF THE MOTHER

Copyright © 1995 by Maria Eftimiades.

Front cover: photograph of Susan Smith by Jonathan Tedder, *Rock Hill Herald* / Sygma. Photograph of the children © Rhonda Gregory, American Fas Photo / Saba. Back cover photograph of house by Associated Press / *Lima News*, Dave Polcyn.

ISBN: 0-312-95658-4

Printed in the United States of America

St. Martin's Paperbacks edition/February 1995

10 9 8 7 6 5 4 3 2 1

This book is dedicated to the residents of Union, South Carolina, who came together in tragedy and, by their unbending love and faith, showed the nation the true meaning of community. In their hearts, Michael and Alex Smith will live on always.

ACKNOWLEDGMENTS

My thanks to *People* Managing Editor Landon Y. Jones, my editors, Roger Wolmuth, Joe Treen and Jack Friedman, and *People* correspondents Don Sider and Gail Wescott. I also want to express my sincere gratitude to *People* Senior Writer Cynthia Sanz for editing this book and for all of her support.

SINS
of the
MOTHER

[1]

The headlights on the burgundy Mazda Protege cast an eerie glow on the dark waters of John D. Long Lake. Just before nine P.M. the lake was deserted. Those who fished catfish from the basin's murky depths had left hours earlier, piloting their johnboats to the shore as darkness fell. Now, the only noise was the hum of the Mazda as it paused atop a seventy-five-foot-long boat ramp. Moments later, the gravel beneath the Mazda's wheels would crunch as the car slowly began its descent.

It was October 25, 1994, a mild night in Union, South Carolina. In the summer months, the lake was a popular gathering place for the townspeople. Just after daybreak and right before dusk, its banks were dotted with fitness walkers marching along the side of the woods near the lake, nodding and calling out greetings to each other.

During the afternoons, teenagers and couples, and most of all, families with young children covered its shores. But as temperatures dropped and the bland fall breezes turned chilly, the crowds began to thin. Even when the sun shone brightly, there was school and homework, so many more commitments as winter approached.

And so the steady tide of cars continued along Highway 49, connecting Union and Lockhart, with fewer and fewer making the turn and passing the green sign that welcomed guests to John D. Long Lake. Most evenings, once darkness enveloped the lake there would be no visitors at all, no sounds again until daybreak.

Yet that night in Union, South Carolina, at John D. Long Lake, a visitor named Susan Smith fractured the quiet.

It was about 8:45 P.M. and Susan sat motionless in the Mazda, her hands clutching the steering wheel. She could hear the rhythmic breathing of her two children asleep in the back seat, their energy finally drained. Michael's third birthday had been just two weeks earlier, and Alex, fourteen months, had recently taken his first steps alone. How they laughed and tumbled through each day, learning and exploring together.

But now, there was only sleep, the deep, tranquil kind a parent expects in a warm, moving car at night. Indeed, it had taken only a few minutes after Susan buckled them into their car seats, before they had both settled down and drifted off.

Susan Smith, twenty-three, shifted the Mazda into neutral and the car slowly began to roll down the ramp. She stepped on the brake. Then, she pulled the emergency brake up with a swift tug. She stepped outside and stood on the banks of the John D. Long Lake.

She had a decision to make.

It didn't matter how long she stood there—the children were asleep and no one was waiting at home for Susan. She and her husband, David, were amid divorce proceedings. Married at nineteen, they had thought their marriage would last a lifetime but it hadn't worked out that way. In August, David moved out of their small red-brick ranch.

Susan's boyfriend, Tom Findlay, wasn't waiting either. After a brief courtship he had decided that Susan was a little too needy for him, and that he was not ready for a commitment, especially not to a woman with two young children. He'd ended their relationship one week earlier.

On the way to the lake that night, Susan had driven by the Winn-Dixie, the local supermarket, where David worked as an assistant manager. She passed the road that led to Judy and Carol Cathcart's day-care center, where Michael and Alexander played on swing sets and gazed out at the cows grazing in the nearby field. She went by Veterans Park, where she occasionally took her sons to feed breadcrumbs to the ducks in the pond. She drove by Conso, the decorative trimmings factory where she worked as a secretary. She wasn't far from the homes of her mother and stepfather, Linda and Bev, and her brother, Scotty and his wife, Wendy.

They were places and people she once cared about, but now there was nothing, only emptiness and pain. The losses in her life had finally numbered too many; she'd felt the sting of rejection from too many men. The responsibilities of motherhood overwhelmed her.

She wondered if death would relieve the ache inside her.

Susan Smith looked out at the blackness of the lake and it was a blackness that consumed her. She wanted relief, a respite from the misery, the loneliness.

She would take them with her, those sweet little ones in the back seat. They would suffer less with her, she believed, than left on their own in a compassionless world without her.

But something inside her prevented Susan from surrendering herself to the blackness. Standing at the lake that night she discovered she didn't want to die: all she wanted was to break from the heavy burden she felt so overwhelmed her. For a moment, nothing else mattered—not even the love Susan had for her children.

In that instant, Susan Leigh Vaughan Smith, whom everyone would later recall as a pretty, intelligent, popular, churchgoing young lady, made the decision that would catapult her into a worldwide spotlight, an odious decision that she would relive again and again.

All the innocence of childhood ended in a moment. Susan reached inside the car and somehow resisted the soft, guileless faces of her little boys.

She alone knows if she said good-bye.

What she did next is what will never be forgotten, or understood. Susan Smith pressed the head of the Mazda's emergency brake and gently lowered the handle down. As the car began to roll, Susan gave the door a push. It slammed shut, sealing the Protege and the fate of Michael and Alexander Smith with a hollow thud.

If Susan Smith stood at the shore of the lake and watched, she likely saw the car drift into John D. Long Lake. Because it entered the dark waters slowly, it didn't submerge immediately. For a few minutes it seemed as if it would just remain there, bobbing endlessly, peacefully. But of course it could not. And as the burgundy Mazda gradually filled with the water from John D. Long Lake, the trust of a mother's heart drowned.

But now, it was too late for regrets. Standing

on the banks of the lake Susan Smith made her next tortured choice: self-preservation. She turned her back on the sinking car and began to run up the road, screaming. The lights of a small house flickered in front of her.

The story she was about to tell would kindle the sympathy of a nation. It would raise doubts in some and bruise a community that prided itself on racial harmony. And it would introduce to the world the faces of two little boys and mobilize a vigorous search to bring them safely home.

When the truth was at last revealed, the world would imagine what happened the night Susan Smith took the lives of her children, replaying the scene at the lake in Union, South Carolina in their minds again and again. Worst of all, both those who knew Michael and Alexander Smith and those who had never met them would hear the sounds inside the Mazda Protege resounding in their hearts for a long time to come.

The question that remained echoed in every small town and every big city: How could she do it? And nowhere was that question pondered more vigorously than in Union, South Carolina, a city that loved Susan Smith, and the two little boys she bore.

She did, the people said, the unthinkable. In one instant, Susan Leigh Vaughan Smith crushed humanity's most sacred trust, the love of a mother for her children.

It was the sin that would test Union's faith that theirs was a forgiving God.

[2]

Shirley McCloud turned the page of the *Union Daily Times* and adjusted the pillow at her head. She had been lying on the living room couch in her thermal nightgown for the past hour, half-listening to the television as she flipped through a stack of newspapers at her feet. It felt good to relax. Shirley left her small, two bedroom house in Union County each morning at 7:00 A.M., driving about thirty miles to her job as a secretary in Spartanburg. She liked her work, but at times, the commute was grueling.

Shirley glanced at the domed brass clock that sat atop the dark wood stand. It was a few minutes past nine. Her husband, Rick, lay on an adjoining sofa, engrossed in a sitcom. Their only child, Rick Jr., twenty-three, was in his bedroom, also watching television.

Well, if I'm going to watch a movie, I need to

see what's on, Shirley thought. She was just about to commandeer the remote control from Rick when she heard a loud disturbance on the porch. She sat up abruptly.

It was a moaning, almost a wailing sound. Shirley wasn't sure what it was. She caught her husband's eye. The banging on the front door took them both by surprise. In the four years they'd lived there the McClouds always used the side entrance.

The *Union Daily Times* dropped to the floor as Shirley McCloud rushed to the door, her husband right behind her. She quickly unfastened the lock, made sure the chain was securely in place, and opened the door a crack.

In the haze of the porch light stood Susan Smith, hysterically sobbing. Shirley immediately unfastened the chain and pulled open the door, the screen door still locked.

"Please help me! Please help me!" Susan wailed.

Shirley peered past Susan to the far end of the porch, her mind racing. Could this be a ruse? Was this woman a decoy for a robber?

"Please help me!" Susan sobbed. "He's got my kids and he's got my car!"

The terror in Susan's voice left no room for doubt. Shirley McCloud hastily unlocked the screen door and reached toward Susan. She wrapped her arms around the young girl's shoulders and pulled her into the house, practically carrying her across the living room. Susan's shrill cries echoed through the little house as she fell back on to the sofa.

"Please tell me again what you said," Shirley said, trying to stay calm.

Susan Smith could barely speak. She gasped, "A black man has got my kids and my car."

Rick McCloud stared at the young woman sobbing hysterically on the couch. He turned and yelled toward the back bedroom, "Rick Junior, call 911!"

The younger McCloud reached for the cordless phone in his room and quickly punched in the numbers.

"Union County Communication" the dispatcher said.

A flustered Rick Jr. tried to explain. "Yes, ma'am," he said. "There's a lady that come up to our door, and she—some guy jumped into—a red light with her car and two kids in it. And he took off, and she got out of the car here at our house."

"And he's got the kids?"

"Yes, ma'am, and her car. I don't—she's real hysterical, and I just decided I need to call the law and get them down here."

The dispatcher called Union County deputy sheriffs to respond, logging in the call at 9:12 P.M. As Rick Jr. emerged from the bedroom and returned the phone to its cradle, his father grabbed the keys to the family's 1993 Pontiac

Bonneville. "Let's go see if we can find them," he said.

As father and son headed out the side door, Shirley McCloud continued to try to calm her visitor. She knelt in front of Susan and took her face in her hands. Susan's skin was wet and clammy, her breaths coming in shallow gasps.

"Now tell me what happened," Shirley said gently.

In a fresh rush of tears, Susan began to tell her story. "A black man stopped me at a red light," she said. "I was stopped at the red light at Monarch and a black man jumped in and told me to drive. I asked him why was he doing this and he said shut up and drive."

Susan's sobs grew louder. "He made me stop right past the sign. I remember I had just passed that sign."

Shirley held Susan's face and tilted it toward her. "What sign?" she asked.

"The John Long sign," said Susan.

The sign, Shirley McCloud knew, was just a few hundred yards outside their front door, directly opposite the turnoff for the lake. On both sides, Highway 49 was lined with thick trees.

"He told me to get out," Susan went on. "He made me stop in the middle of the road. Nobody was coming, not a single car."

Shirley McCloud listened intently. Her mind was racing. *What a dangerous spot to stop a car, in the middle of the road,* she thought. *And no cars around at all? God, if there had been a car somebody would have helped her.*

Susan continued her story. "I asked him, 'Why can't I take my kids?' But he said, 'I don't have time.' He kept pushing me out of the car, pointing a gun at my side."

Shirley tried to envision the scene. "Did he get out and go around the car?" she asked.

"No, he kept pushing me out the door," Susan said quickly. "When he finally got me out he said, 'Don't worry, I'm not going to hurt your kids.' I dropped to the ground. I don't know how long I sat there. Then I got up and started running and I saw your house."

Shirley held Susan's head in her hands. At the top of her head was a large white bow, her light brown hair scooped back in a high pony tail. *Such a pretty young girl,* Shirley thought. *So frail.*

"Do you feel faint?" she asked.

"No," Susan said. "But I need to go to the bathroom."

Shirley helped Susan stand. Holding her shoulders tightly, she led her to the light gray bathroom in between the two bedrooms. As she waited outside the door, Shirley wondered how soon the police would arrive.

Susan emerged a few seconds later. "I've got to call my Momma," she announced.

Shirley reached for the cordless phone. "I'll

dial it for you," she said. Susan returned to the sofa and in a halting voice, recited her mother's telephone number. Shirley pressed the buttons and listened as it rang. A young man answered. It was Susan's oldest brother, Michael, who lived at home.

"This is Shirley McCloud," she said, her voice quavering. "I live near John D. Long Lake on Route 49. I have Susan Smith in my home. Is Susan's mother there?"

"She just left," he said.

Shirley turned to Susan. "Your mother's not there," she said.

Susan's sobs grew louder. "Tell Michael he's got to find her," she said.

Shirley returned to the phone. "Can you get her?" she asked. "A black man has taken her kids and her car. There's no way you can find her mother?"

On the other end of the phone, Shirley heard a gasp. "I'll try," Michael said.

When Shirley hung up Susan motioned for the phone. "I need to call my stepfather, too," she said.

Susan tried to make the call herself, but her hands were shaking too much. "I'll do it," Shirley told her, taking the phone.

When Susan told her the name of her stepfather, Shirley was surprised. She knew of Bev Russell. Everyone in town did. For many years, Bev had run a profitable business, Bev's TV and

Appliance store, in downtown Union. He had closed it just a few months previously, and began working as an investment-and-tax advisor. Bev was active in local politics and the Christian community.

Bev Russell answered right away and Shirley quickly explained who she was. "I have Susan Smith here who says a black man has taken her kids and her car."

She heard him exhale sharply. "What?" Bev practically shouted. "What did you say and who are you and where do you live?"

Shirley repeated the story. She handed the phone to Susan, who tearfully told her stepfather the story of the black man, the gun, the kidnapping of her children. Bev Russell promised his stepdaughter he would be there as soon as possible.

Susan asked to go to the bathroom a second time. Shirley went to the linen closet and pulled out a white washcloth. She soaked it in cool water.

When Susan emerged again, she was slightly calmer. There was one more phone call to make.

"I need to call my husband, David," she told Shirley McCloud. "He works at Winn-Dixie."

For the third time in less than ten minutes, Shirley McCloud explained who she was and told the story of the black man taking Susan Smith's children and car. As she spoke, David kept saying, "What? What?" Then, "Okay.

Okay. Okay. I'm coming. I'm coming. I'm coming."

About eight miles away, Sheriff Howard Wells had just finished leading a planning meeting for his second-in-command, Captain of the Patrol Division Roger Gregory and Harry Helms, supervisor of the reserve program. The men discussed new possibilities within the department's ten-member reserve unit and the likelihood of buying new equipment. When it was over Wells turned out the lights, locked the door to his office and to the outside. The office of the sheriff's department closes at 5:00 P.M., when his four secretaries go home. From that point on, calls are handled through dispatchers at the Union County Communications Building and by the Union County Police Department.

Howard Wells walked across the parking lot to his car. He was tired. He had left his brick ranch home with a red shingle roof on the north side of town shortly after eight A.M., some twelve hours earlier. He had known it would be a long day. That morning, he had told his wife, Wanda, that he would grab dinner out before the reserve meeting and probably be home around nine. Wanda understood. She always did.

As Wells pulled out of the parking lot he turned left on Highway 49, heading for Highway 176 for the five-minute drive home. As he drove, he listened to his deputies talking to a dispatcher on the scanner.

His men sounded agitated. *Something must be going on,* he thought. Because he'd missed the initial call from the dispatcher he couldn't quite figure out what the problem was. He continued to drive, trying to catch the gist of the situation. He listened for a moment more, then reached for his microphone.

"What kind of call do you have?" he asked.

The deputy sheriff recognized Well's voice and answered quickly.

"A car was taken from a woman at gun point," he said.

Wells continued toward home. He was surprised—a carjacking in Union? It had never happened before. Regardless, his deputies could handle that, he thought. Wells had been elected Union County's sheriff almost two years before, taking on a staff of twenty-five full-time deputies, ten unpaid reserve deputies and four office clerks. He had trained his staff well and had a lot of faith in them.

Wells was just nearing the turn onto Highway 176 when he heard the deputy speaking to the dispatcher.

"Advise. Did you say children were involved?"

"Yes, children were in the car."

Sheriff Wells hit the brake and the car stopped with a jolt. He grabbed the microphone.

"I'll stop at the home," he told the deputies on

the frequency, his voice strong. "Start systematic patrol of the area. I'll relay the information as fast as I get it."

By 9:15 P.M. dozens of deputy sheriffs, city police, and family and friends of Susan Smith were speeding up Highway 49, en route to Shirley and Rick McCloud's little house just opposite the road leading to John D. Long Lake.

At the same time, Rick McCloud and his son were maneuvering their Bonneville around the lake itself. While Shirley McCloud had stayed behind to try and comfort Susan until the police and her family arrived, the men had decided to begin their own search for the missing children. They had driven straight to the lake in the hopes that Susan's carjacker might have decided that the deserted shores would be an easy place to abandon the children and make a clean getaway with the Mazda.

"Maybe the guy let them out down there," Rick had told his son. "I hope we find the kids."

It took only a few seconds for the men to reach the dead end. The headlights of the Bonneville shone down the boat launch at the still and silent lake. Rick McCloud and his son gazed into the dark waters at the same spot Susan Smith had sat in her Mazda Protege, her little boys strapped securely in the back seat, less than twenty minutes earlier. The faint signs of tire tracks were embedded in the gravel leading to the water. But it was too dark to see them.

Besides, who would believe it possible?

Indeed, there was nothing to see from the banks of the lake, and no sounds at all. By now, the Mazda had drifted out 100 feet, overturned and settled into a depression amidst the algae bloom and silt eighteen feet below. The McCloud men looked for just a moment more, and then turned and drove back home.

The children, they believed, were not there. There were no answers, the men thought sadly, at the lake that night.

[3]

When Rick and his son returned from the lake they settled down on a porch swing on the side deck to wait for the police.

By then, Susan Smith had calmed down slightly. She told Shirley McCloud where she lived, and that she and David had separated several months before and were getting a divorce. Just before the police arrived Susan asked Shirley McCloud if she had any children.

"Yes, I've got that big boy out there on the deck," Shirley said, motioning to Rick Jr.

Susan nodded. She glanced at an eight-by-ten framed photograph on the table of a pretty, dark-haired girl. "That's my son's girlfriend," Shirley said.

Susan then asked if the McClouds were related to a McCloud she knew. They weren't, Shirley told her, but she knew the person Susan meant. Weeks later, Shirley thought back to that brief exchange. "If my son were missing I can't imagine I'd care about anything else," she recalled.

The first officers arrived at the McCloud house within a few minutes of the 911 call. Questions flew. "What direction did he go? What kind of car?"

Sheriff Wells was next at the scene. Another patrol car, directly behind him, sped off down Highway 49, looking for the Mazda with a black man at the wheel and two babies in the back seat. The deputies drove almost into the next county, searching.

When Sheriff Wells entered the McCloud house everyone turned to him. He nodded to his deputies. "Go ahead and look," he told them. "I'll take the report."

The men hurried to their patrol cars and Wells turned to the young woman sobbing on the sofa. He was surprised but didn't show it. He'd known Susan for years, and knew members of her family well. Wells's wife Wanda was close friends with Wendy Vaughan, the wife of Susan's brother Scotty. The two women had met several years earlier, when both were working at Union Federal Savings Bank, just across from the Union County Courthouse. They became fast friends, and, with the passage of time, their husbands, too, had grown close.

Over the years the two couples often double-dated, and visited each other's homes for dinners and parties. When Scotty and Wendy's two children were baptized, they asked Wanda and Howard to be godparents. At Vaughan family functions, the Wellses had seen Susan and her two little boys. And when Susan and David bought their small ranch house on Toney Road, they lived just across the city's new four-lane highway from the Wells, about three blocks north.

Susan Smith looked very different now, her hair askew, her face white and streaked with tears. Her hands shook uncontrollably. Sheriff Wells knelt before her.

"I'm going to have to start getting some details, Susan," he said gently. "You need to tell me what happened."

By now, Wells had already heard the story from the dispatchers, and from the McClouds. None of that mattered. He wanted to hear it from Susan.

Susan began to talk, telling her tale once more. As the story unfolded, Wells asked questions and jotted down her answers. He continuously relayed bits of information over the radio to his deputies on the road.

As time passed, Wells began to realize that this situation was not going to clear up quickly. He called for assistance from the highway patrol and asked a dispatcher to patch him through with Chief Robert Stewart, the head of South Carolina Law Enforcement Division, known as SLED.

As unusual as the carjacking report was for Union County, Sheriff Howard Wells had no reason to doubt Susan Smith's story. Wells was a seasoned lawman. The first step in any police investigation, he knew, was simply to gather all the available information and follow whatever leads presented themselves. Any detail might be the one that would solve the case and bring those little boys home. Only later, with more time to examine all the available evidence and rule things out by fact could he question the information he'd been given.

It was a cardinal rule of law enforcement, and Wells respected it.

Shortly after Sheriff Wells arrived, members of Susan's family began to show up. Her mother, Linda, and stepfather, Bev, their faces drawn with worry, rushed in to hug her. When David arrived he gathered his estranged wife in his arms, practically carrying her. Shirley McCloud couldn't help but notice as she watched the young couple trying to comfort each other; they looked so loving, so close.

Susan's brother Scotty and his wife Wendy arrived, as well as Susan's best friend, Donna Garner, and her parents. At one point Susan's mother, Linda, slipped out the front door and stood silently on the porch, alone.

As Sheriff Wells continued to question Susan, her stepfather, Bev Russell, asked Shirley McCloud for a phone. She handed him the cordless, and he called the Reverend Mark Long, the pastor of Buffalo United Methodist Church, just three miles west of Union.

Reverend Long was new to Union County—he had come from a church in Lancaster, South Carolina in June—but in his four months in Buffalo had clearly impressed his 360-member congregation—including Bev Russell. Bev was one of the church's most active members. He attended services faithfully every Sunday and even sang in the church choir.

That night at the McClouds', Bev Russell told the minister of the bizarre story concerning his stepdaughter and her missing children. Shirley McCloud felt a wave of sadness as she overheard Bev quietly ask his pastor for help.

"Please start the prayers," Bev said.

Reverend Long promised he would.

Throughout the city of Union, news of the carjacking and the missing boys spread like a brushfire. The *Union Daily Times* photographer, Tim Kimzey, heard deputies discussing the search on the police scanner as they explored little-known country roads off Highway 49. Kimzey, on staff at the newspaper for more than a year, didn't bother to call his editor: he just grabbed his camera and went directly to the McCloud home.

A carjacking in Union, two missing babies, a hysterical young mother. This story, he knew, would be on Page One in the next day's edition.

Over on Toney Road, Susan's neighbor, Dot Frost, was getting the news, too. Dot, sixty-three, also had a police scanner on in her bedroom. But unlike Kimzey, for Dot, listening to the scanner was a hobby. She liked to know what was going on around town. That night, when Dot caught the agitated voices of the deputies, she perched on the edge of her bed and tried to figure out what was going on.

In a few minutes, she put together the story. She called out to her son, Scott, twenty-three, who was watching television in the living room. "I hear there was a carjacking at Monarch at the red light," she said. "I don't see how. Every time you go there the cars are coming two different ways. It doesn't stay red for more than a second."

Dot Frost walked into the living room and glanced out the small window on top of the front door. It was late now, past ten P.M. Across the street, Susan Smith's small house was dark, her burgundy Mazda Protege not in the driveway.

How odd, Dot thought. *She's got those two babies to bring in the house. She always leaves the outside light on when she's going to be late.*

Dot turned to her son. "Susan's light's not on," she said. "Maybe she spent the night somewhere?"

Scott just shrugged. He had known Susan for years. They'd been in the same graduating class at Union High School and had worked side by side as cashiers at Winn-Dixie, the local supermarket. Even now, they both worked for the same company, Conso, a decorative trimmings factory, just a mile up Highway 176. Still, Scott Frost knew her only to say hello, and that was about it.

Dot couldn't stop wondering why Susan wasn't home. She knew quite a bit about her neighbors. It was easy to tell when Susan and David were having trouble: more than once Dot peered through the curtains of her living room window as David packed and moved out. She'd seen his bedroom set moved in and out twice by now.

But this seemed unusual. Susan always left the house around eight A.M., strapping her little boys into their car seats, and driving to the babysitter. In the evening, the Mazda pulled into the driveway around 5:30. Dot always smiled when she'd see them return home. Susan would unstrap the boys and lift them out of the car. She'd carry little Alex, and hand Michael the diaper bag. It was sweet to watch them trudge into the house, Michael dragging the diaper bag on the ground behind him.

Two blocks up Toney Road, on the other side of Highway 176, Sheriff Howard Wells's wife, Wanda, first heard the news on the police scanner she always left on in the kitchen. She had been watching television in the living room, waiting patiently for her husband. As long as she'd known him he'd been in law enforcement and long days and phone calls in the middle of the night were routine.

Suddenly, she heard a brisk exchange on the scanner. She heard her husband's voice, and then "100"—his call number.

Wanda Wells grabbed the remote control and lowered the volume on the television. She couldn't quite make out what had happened, something about a car, something about the Monarch red light. Then she heard her husband say he was responding to the call. Wanda sat at the kitchen table and tried to figure out who the deputies were talking about. Carjacking and kidnappings just didn't happen in Union, she thought.

She realized she probably wouldn't see her husband until morning. Little did she know that for the next nine days she would see him more at televised press conferences than at home.

Wanda met Howard Wells in 1975, when he

was a twenty-four-year-old Union city cop, and she, a twenty-year-old bank employee, one year out of Union High School. They had both grown up in Union but their paths had never crossed. At the time, Wanda was engaged, but her brother, William Jolly, a Union County deputy sheriff, didn't like the young man. Jolly shrewdly arranged for his little sister to meet his friend Howard Wells.

A short time later, much to Jolly's delight, Wanda broke her engagement. She and Howard Wells began dating in February, 1976 and were engaged four months later. They married in May, 1977.

The following June, Howard Wells left the city police and joined the sheriff's department as a deputy. For four years, he worked side by side with Jolly. Then, in the fall of 1980, William Jolly ran for sheriff of Union County and won. In February, 1980, a month after Jolly began serving his term, Howard Wells quit the department, concerned that it would appear to be a conflict of interest for him to work for his brother-in-law.

Wells took a position as a conservation officer with the South Carolina Department of Natural Resources and for the next twelve years he helped enforce game, fishing, and boating laws for the state. State conservation officers also assist all other law enforcement agencies because of their access to four-wheel drive trucks and various watercrafts. They are used in special detail work to provide protection for visiting dignitaries, and for weather and other related disasters.

In 1992, William Jolly announced that he would not run for another term, having already served three four-year terms. Howard Wells then ran for sheriff and won. Jolly took a job with SLED.

All these law enforcement men in her life had helped Wanda Wells be accepting of the pressures and uncertainties the job entailed. She knew how much the sheriff's department meant to her husband and brother. In some ways, law enforcement was her life, too.

The ringing of the telephone interrupted her thoughts. It was Martha Jolly, William's wife. The Jollys lived right on Highway 49, about three miles south of John D. Long Lake.

Martha told Wanda that William had been called to help search for the carjacker. She asked Wanda if she knew the young woman whose children had been taken.

"I didn't catch the name," Wanda said.

"I didn't either," Martha replied. "I've been listening since William's been gone but I haven't gotten anything."

As they chatted, the two women half-listened to their scanners. Both knew their husbands were not likely to come home anytime soon.

* * *

At Shirley and Rick McCloud's home, some forty family members and friends of Susan and David Smith gathered to try and comfort the young couple. More than ten sheriff's deputies tramped in and out of the house, getting orders and fanning out in the area in search of the missing Mazda and Susan's boys. At one point, Shirley McCloud wondered if they were going to set up a command post in her living room and stay all night. Once Sheriff Wells had gently suggested to Susan that they move to another place, but Susan seemed reluctant.

Around eleven P.M., two hours after a hysterical Susan Smith appeared on the McCloud's porch, Sheriff Wells began making plans to move the search operation.

"We need to leave this family's home," he told Susan more firmly. "You need to decide, Susan, where you want to set up so I can have easy access to you."

The room was silent. Then Susan spoke. "I want to go to my Momma's," she said, a catch in her throat."

"Okay," Wells said. "We need to leave then."

The deputies headed to their patrol cars, and one by one, the family and friends of Susan Smith thanked Shirley and Rick McCloud. When Susan reached the door, Shirley hugged her tightly.

"I'm so sorry," Shirley whispered.

"Thank you," Susan whispered back. "Thank you so much."

When the last person had left, Shirley, Rick, and Rick Jr. stood in the living room and looked at each other. The house, which had been bustling with activity all evening, was suddenly quiet. Shirley thought about how she had managed to stay in control of her emotions for two hours. Not long after the door closed and the last car pulled out of the driveway, she broke down and cried.

As the deputies continued the search for the car, the family headed to the home of Susan's mother and stepfather. It was a sprawling ranch house on Heathwood Road in the affluent Mount Vernon Estates section of Union. Not long after they arrived, Tim Kimzey knocked at the door.

He explained that he was a photographer for the Union newspaper and that he wanted to run a picture of the missing children in the next day's edition. Kimzey had already been down to John D. Long Lake, shooting pictures of the deputies searching the woods. At the Russell home, Linda and Bev welcomed him enthusiastically, leading him into the den.

They introduced him to Susan and David, and gave him a four-by-six print of the two boys, of Michael sitting in a white wicker chair, and little Alex on his lap. Both were smiling. Kimzey carefully clicked off several shots of the photograph. Then he asked to photograph Susan and David.

"Should I take my glasses off?" Susan asked.

Kimzey tried not to look surprised. He couldn't imagine how a mother who'd just lost her two children could care about her appearance.

"Whatever feels comfortable for you," he managed to say.

Susan pulled off her glasses, and settled back on the sofa next to David. Kimzey asked the young couple to hold up a picture of their sons, and for the next thirty minutes he shot a roll of film of the distraught pair. It was after midnight when he left. He thought how fortunate it was that the Union paper was published in the afternoons. There was plenty of time to make the noon deadline.

Once Susan and David were settled in at the Russell home, Sheriff Wells headed back to his office, and the enormous task of planning investigation strategies began. He needed to get a better description of the suspect from Susan and arrange for a police artist to sketch a composite drawing. He had to coordinate with SLED and call in divers to check John D. Long Lake.

Back on Toney Road, his wife, Wanda, was waiting anxiously for more information about the case. Martha Jolly called once more around midnight.

"Have you heard anything more?" she asked.

"No, I'm still listening," Wanda told her.

Martha had news. She'd gotten a phone call from a friend who had heard the name of the victim. "I heard it was Susan Smith," Martha said.

"Susan Smith, Susan Smith, Susan Smith," Wanda said, thinking aloud. "That name sounds so familiar. I should know her. I know I should know her."

After she hung up, Wanda listened on and off to the scanner, napping on the couch. Finally, at two A.M., she turned it off and went to bed. She was an assistant vice president at Union Federal Savings bank and had to be in early the next morning.

Wanda Wells slept fitfully. She wondered about her husband, when he would come home. She couldn't stop thinking about the missing children.

Neither could Shirley McCloud. She lay awake next to her husband, unable to sleep at all. Images of Susan Smith, hysterical on her front porch, kept flashing through her mind. All night, Shirley heard the whirling sounds of the SLED helicopter flying above her house, and over the woods surrounding John D. Long Lake.

Where are those babies? she kept thinking. *Where are they?*

[4]

Some people's lives are grounded in deception. For Susan Smith, maintaining the image of the model daughter, friend, wife, and mother was an arduous, lifelong task. And in the end, it collapsed, her terrible secrets rising to the surface.

Susan was born in Union on September 26, 1971, the only daughter of Linda, a homemaker, and Harry Ray Vaughan, a firefighter who later worked as a winder at a textile mill. Linda had a son, Michael, whom they called Moe, from a previous relationship, and with Harry, another son, Scotty. The Vaughans lived in a modest brick house on Siegler Road, just outside downtown Union. In was near Foster Park Elementary School where Susan was a student. When she was a little girl, Susan always wore pretty dresses to the classroom, her light brown hair pulled back in fancy bows. She shined in grade school, bright and eager to learn.

But life at home on Siegler Road was far from harmonious. In 1977, after seventeen years of marriage, Linda Vaughan asked her husband for a divorce. Susan was six years old.

Harry Vaughan, devastated by the breakup of his marriage, moved into an apartment in a nearby housing development and began drinking heavily at a local bar, Alias Smith & Jones. He'd show up with friends for half-price beers during Happy Hour every day around four P.M.

"He was outgoing and good-looking—a sweet and nice guy," recalls a woman who tended bar there. "Everyone liked him."

The Vaughans' divorce became final on December 7, 1977. Five weeks later, on January 15, 1978, Harry Vaughan took a gun and shot himself in the stomach.

Many believe that Harry Vaughan did not intend to kill himself, but rather hoped his suicide attempt would draw attention to his pain and perhaps reconcile his family. In fact, moments after he pulled the trigger, Harry Vaughan called for help. But it was too late, and Harry died. It was two months before his thirty-fifth birthday.

Shortly after Harry's death, Linda Vaughan married Beverly Russell, a wealthy businessman who owned an appliance store in downtown Union. Bev, who had several daughters from a previous marriage, was well-known in Union. A longtime Democrat who had ultimately switched to the Republican party, he had become a state Republican executive committeeman, as well as a member of the advisory board of the Christian Coalition.

After her mother remarried, Susan and her brothers moved from the cozy Siegler Road home to their new stepfather's large three-bedroom ranch house with a big yard in the more exclusive Mount Vernon Estates section of Union.

Little Susan held tight to memories of her father. She often listened to a cassette tape of her dad laughing as he tried to teach her to talk when she was a toddler. She kept an eight-by-ten photograph of him in the bottom of her desk drawer at home, next to a coin collection he had given her.

Harry Vaughan was buried at the edge of Union Memorial Gardens Perpetual Care Cemetery on Highway 176, a few miles from Bev Russell's home. From the car, Susan could see her father's grave as they rode past almost every day.

Susan's childhood friend, Stacey Hartley, recalls those years as particularly hard on Susan. "I remember when her daddy died. It was during the winter and there was snow on the ground," says Hartley. "I turned on the radio and they said he shot himself. Susan took it hard. I remember Susan crying and all. I remember crying myself when her mother remarried and they moved to Mount Vernon. I went up to her new house and stayed with her every now and then, but it was never the same as those days in the hammock, this hammock in Susan's yard. We used to swing in that hammock and laugh and laugh."

Susan earned good grades throughout elementary school and junior high, and later, at Union High School, she seemed to excell at everything. She was a member of the Beta Club, a group for students with higher than a B average, as well as a member of the Math, Spanish, and Red Cross Clubs. She volunteered to help put on the city's annual Special Olympics competition, and did work with the elderly. Susan was named president of the Junior Civitan Club, an outreach organization, and from 1986 to 1988, she and her best friend, Donna Garner, worked as candy stripers at Wallace Thomson Hospital in downtown Union.

In her senior year in 1989, Susan Leigh Vaughan was voted Friendliest Female at Union High School. Her classmates say she always smiled, was always cheerful and down to earth. Slightly husky and five feet, three inches tall, Susan usually wore miniskirts and blouses, flattering her figure.

"All the guys wanted Susan," remembers

Kenny Jennings, who went to school with Susan and later worked with her at Winn-Dixie. "We thought of her like a model, a real nice-looking girl, a nice build. I'm surprised she didn't get Best Looking in our class."

Despite the perfect appearance, there was turmoil in Susan's life. In 1988, when she was seventeen, she appeared at the office of the high school's guidance counselor, Camille Stribling, and said she had been molested by her stepfather, Bev Russell. By law, school officials are required to report child abuse allegations. Stribling called the State Department of Social Services. An official there called the Union County Sheriff's Office.

In early 1989, when the sheriff at the time, William Jolly, attempted to investigate the molestation charges, Susan and her mother, Linda, said they did not want to pursue it any further. Ultimately, there was never a court hearing in the case. Judge David Wilburn was presented with an agreement hammered out between Russell's attorney, Robert Guess, and Assistant Sixteenth Circuit Solicitor Jack Flynn. The judge sealed the court records on March 25, 1988.

Despite the claims of abuse, Susan continued to strive. She began working part-time after school at Winn-Dixie. She started as a cashier, but within six months, had moved up to head cashier, and then bookkeeper. She made friends easily and was well liked by her co-workers at the supermarket.

"Most of the time girls didn't stock the shelves, but Susan was the kind of girl who didn't mind stepping in and helping the guys out," recalled Jennings. "She worked so good she moved up very quickly. Everyone knew Susan was trying to succeed, trying to get ahead. She deserved it."

It was at Winn-Dixie that Susan got to know David Smith, whom she knew casually from high school, where he had been one year ahead of her. David, who grew up in nearby Putman, didn't smoke or drink and worked long hours at the supermarket, beginning when he was just sixteen years old.

At first, the two were simply friends. David was dating his longtime girlfriend, Kristy, and Susan had begun seeing someone as well. In her senior year, when Susan was eighteen years old, she started secretly dating an older married man. "No one was supposed to know," a former co-worker said. "But the guy would tell me and David about it, and we could see it."

About that time, Susan became pregnant and had an abortion. Thereafter, the relationship ended. Deeply depressed, Susan took an overdose of aspirin and Anacin.

She was admitted to Spartanburg Regional Medical Center from November 7 to November 15, 1989, not long after the start of her senior year of high school. In the hospital, doctors discovered that this wasn't Susan's first attempt at suicide. She had taken a similar aspirin overdose when she was only thirteen years old.

News of Susan's suicide attempt traveled quickly at the high school and at Winn-Dixie. Her managers at the store were supportive, telling her that she was welcome to return to work whenever she was ready. She took about a month off from school and work, and then went back.

By then, David Smith's interest in the pretty bookkeeper had grown. At the time, he was a stock clerk in the dairy and frozen-foods section. He broke up with Kristy, and set his sights on Susan.

He talked to his friend Kenny about it. "He said he liked her and I told him, 'David, it's going to be hard to get her; you're not good enough,'" Kenny recalled. "I was shocked when they hooked up. David just jumped in. He had confidence that he could have her. They became real good friends, and a month later he was taking her home from work. A year later they were married."

In many ways, marrying David Smith seemed to be the remedy to all the sorrow in Susan Vaughan's life. Now, she would have her own family and the protected, stable environment she so craved. For no one, it seemed to Susan, had loved her enough before.

David Michael Smith, was born July 27, 1970 in Michigan. By the time he turned two the family moved to Putman, about five miles northwest of Union. His father, Charles David Smith, also called David, worked for a while in Harry From's clothing store in downtown Union, and eventually took a job as manager of a Wal-Mart. David's mother, Barbara, worked on and off in a lawyer's office and in a dialysis clinic. She also went to school part-time to study nursing.

David had a half-brother, Billy, from his mother's first marriage, an older brother, Danny, and a younger sister, Becky. David and Danny were particularly close, playing football with the neighborhood kids, and exploring in the nearby woods.

Growing up, the Smith children joined their parents at weekly Jehovah's Witness meetings at Kingdom Hall in Union on Route 18. By age sixteen, however, David broke from his parents' religion, causing friction within the family. He moved in with his great grandmother, Forest Malone, who lived next door.

After school, David worked hard at Winn-Dixie. Eventually, he moved up to assistant manager, handling most of the customer service, usually working the 3:00 to 11:00 P.M. shift. David, said Jennings, was always willing to help stocking shelves, or doing anything else that was needed. "Everybody loves him," said Jennings. "He's the best manager there. He always helps out. He always stays on top of everybody but he doesn't jump down your throat. He'll say, 'I need you to do this.' We'd always laugh and joke, call each other funny names."

One co-worker recalled that in 1987, when a fellow co-worker was close to getting fired, David talked to his boss, encouraging him to give the young man another chance. It was one of many kindnesses his co-workers recall. "If somebody shows up at closing and needs Pampers, he'll let them in," one said. "He's that kind of guy."

After David and Susan had been dating for a year, Susan became pregnant.

On Valentine's Day, 1991, Susan and David filled out a marriage license. A month later, on March 15, 1991, they were wed at United Methodist Church in Bogansville. Susan was nineteen, David, twenty.

After the wedding, as they prepared to drive away, Susan waved to her family and friends. "I love y'all," she said. Susan then moved in with David at his great-grandmother's house.

A short time later, David mailed a copy of his wedding video to his friend Kenny Jennings, who had by then moved to New York and was unable to attend the wedding. David attached a note saying how happy he was that he and Susan were finally going to be together forever.

But the start of the marriage came at a tumultuous time in the Smith family. David's brother Danny, then twenty-two, a worker for the Buffalo Water Department, was gravely ill with Crone's disease, an acute inflammation of the gastrointestinal tract. In the winter of 1991, Danny had surgery at Spartanburg Regional Medical Center, but bacteria developed and his condition quickly deteriorated. Just eleven days before David and Susan's wedding, Danny Smith died.

The funeral was held at the Bogansville United Methodist Church were Susan and David would later marry. Danny was buried in the cemetery behind the white church. On his stone it read, "Daniel Steven Smith. Feb. 12, 1969–March 4, 1991. Loved by all."

The marriage of David's parents had been rocky, but once Danny died, it quickly fell apart. David's mother, Barbara, moved to Garden City, near Myrtle Beach. David's father, a Navy veteran who had served during the Vietnam War, was crushed by the death of his son and fell into a deep depression.

Not long after Danny's death, Susan walked into her father-in-law's home and found him collapsed on the floor. He had taken an overdose of pills. She called for help and Charles David Smith eventually recovered. The pain of his suicide attempt touched many that knew him.

"A lot of people knew about David's father—it

was so sad," said a woman who worked with him at Wal-Mart. "He was always a sweet, feeling person. It was pretty hard on the department store. It really affected David's family."

And perhaps Susan, too. By nineteen, she had suffered the suicide of her father, twice attempted to kill herself, claimed to have been sexually molested, and stumbled on her father-in-law near death by his own hand.

And then, two weeks after her twentieth birthday, just seven months after her marriage, Susan Vaughan Smith faced the greatest responsibility she'd ever known: she became a mother.

[5]

In the months before giving birth to Michael, Susan Smith was radiant.

"We were pregnant at the same time," recalls Julie Hart, who worked with David's father at Wal-Mart. "I'd see her at Winn-Dixie after my baby was born and she'd say, 'I can't wait for mine.' She was elated. She was so happy, she couldn't wait. She was always in a good mood."

Hart remembers joking with David about the trials of parenthood. "I'd always kid, 'You're going to be up nights, now,' " she said. "He said he didn't care. He said he'd take all the night feedings, he didn't mind."

Susan worked at Winn-Dixie right up until the time she went into labor. On October 10, 1991, Michael Daniel Smith was born at Mary Black Hospital in Spartanburg. The young couple chose his middle name in honor of David's brother Danny.

· Shortly after Michael's birth, Susan wrote this entry in her diary: "It was truly the most wonderful experience of my life. When I heard Michael's first cry I just started crying with him. I was so happy. I had given birth to the most beautiful boy in the world. When he was put in my arms for the very first time, I forgot all about my pain. He really lifted my spirits and touched my heart."

Susan worked part-time at Winn-Dixie and had begun taking a few college courses at the University of South Carolina in Union. When the couple had time together, they took Michael and looked for a house. David's sister Becky and her husband Wallace had just bought a house in Cross Keys, about ten miles from Union, and Susan and David asked their advice on mortgages and home ownership. Sometimes, Becky brought her daughter, Kailly Sabrina, born one day after Michael, over to visit.

In the winter of 1992, the Smiths settled on a small ranch with a brown roof and dark red shutters on Toney Road in the north part of town. The mortgage ran $340 a month.

But not long after they moved in, the marriage ran into trouble. It was no surprise among their friends. In Union, couples traditionally marry young and quickly begin families, often discovering that the demands and responsibilities far exceed their expectations. Coupled with financial worries, many young marriages end swiftly.

And so did the marriage of David and Susan Smith. By their third wedding anniversary, they had separated several times, with David moving out of the Toney Road house and back with his great-grandmother in Putman. Unlike many young couples, the Smiths' greatest difficulty wasn't money troubles; David earned about $22,000 a year, Susan, $17,000. The battle was each other's extramarital affairs.

During the first separation, Susan had rekindled a romance with a former boyfriend, infuriating David. But mostly, sparks flew when David began an affair with a pretty young cashier at Winn-Dixie, Tiffany Moss. His co-workers confirm that David and Tiffany were an item, and that Susan knew about it.

On several occasions, Susan showed up at Winn-Dixie, kids in tow, and lashed into David. "She was very jealous," one cashier recalled. "She would take him to the back and scream at him. He'd come back and tell us, 'Yeah, Susan thinks I'm messing with these girls.' "

Adds another, "If she saw him talking to other girls, she'd get upset."

During one of their reconciliations, Susan became pregnant with Alex. But even after his birth on August 5, 1993, the marriage continued to deteriorate. Co-workers say that during one of the separations Susan caught David in bed with Tiffany Moss.

"She came in screaming, 'I know we're separated, but I'm tired of you screwing around,' " a co-worker recalled.

Yet until the end, David maintained that he wanted to save his marriage to Susan. "He said he wanted to work things out but she didn't want to give it another try," a friend recalled. "He was upset. He said the kids needed a father and a mother. He always said the kids were his main priority and that's all he had to live for."

Adds Susan's friend Stacey Hartley, "You never knew if they were separated or together. But Susan loved David. She really loved him. She took him back plenty of times. You never knew when they were together, when they weren't together."

Indeed, just four months before they separated, David penned a loving third anniversary card to his wife: "Hang in there Sugar Booger. You mean everything to me. God, I love you."

Despite the ups and downs in her marriage, by all accounts, Susan Smith was a devoted mother who adored her children and never raised her voice to them. Neighbors recall how Susan would play with the children in front of the house, pulling Michael in his red wagon.

When she took Michael for his first hair-cut, Susan brought along a camcorder, filming the special event. She comforted him with kisses when he fussed. And after it was over, Susan got on her knees and collected the clipped locks in a small bag.

Michael was especially attached to his mom. He held her hand tightly whenever they went out, and was often too shy to play with neighborhood children if his mother wasn't nearby.

Friends and relatives recall how Susan took the children to have portraits made, handing out copies. "After the babies was born, she always had pictures ready," said her cousin, Mary Hickson, in an interview with Union's radio station, WBCU. "If you asked how her babies was, she could show you pictures."

When her father-in-law worked at Wal-Mart, Susan often brought Michael in to visit. Later, after Alex was born, she'd bring both children by Winn-Dixie several times a week to see their dad, even during their separations. David always took time out to play with the boys. They loved to climb around in the customer service office.

"Susan and David just so much enjoyed being with the children," said Mary Hickson. "When the kids needed anything, to go to the doctor, or anything, David was always there. No matter what kind of problem they were having they always worked with the children. That was their goal. That's the one thing they didn't have a problem with."

Now and then, Susan would stop in at a nearby clothing store in the same shopping center. "She'd come in shopping with kids," recalled a young woman who worked in the store, "and she'd always smile. It didn't matter who it was—she smiled. It was so natural for her."

The sales clerk recalled how caring little Michael was toward his brother. "If the baby cried, Michael would say, 'It's going to be all right,' " she said. "You'd see the babies walking along, holding hands."

Susan also made sure the children were happy at their day care. She arranged to take them to Judy and Carol Cathcart's grey shingle house at the end of a dead-end street in Buffalo, about three miles from home. Every morning Susan shuffled the boys past the yellow "Beware of Kids" on the front door and kissed them goodbye. Michael and Alex loved to point to the cows in the fenced-in yard, and to play with the other children on the outdoor swing set.

On Sundays, Susan usually took her sons to church at Buffalo Methodist, attending the same service as her mother and stepfather. Throughout the service, little Alex stayed in the nursery, happily playing on the orange plastic slide. Michael, however, was old enough to attend the part of the service geared toward children. He would toddle down the aisle, past his mother and grandparents, and sit at Reverend Long's knee at the altar. He listened patiently as the minister gave the squirming children a brief lesson from the Bible.

Wilma Brawley took care of Michael and Alex in the church nursery. She, too, recalled Susan as a loving mother. "They loved her and she loved them back," said Wilma, on WBCU. "Any time they cried, if we couldn't get 'em hushed, we'd go get the mother. She'd come right in. The children would stop crying just the minute she walked in the door. She'd sit on the floor and play with them in the nursery and they were just as happy as they could be. They just always wanted their mother with them."

In the summer of 1994, Susan and David discussed the terms of divorce, and a few days before Alex's first birthday party, David moved out. He rented a two-bedroom apartment in the white-shingled Lakeside Gardens complex about two miles from the Toney Road house. He stopped in at Heilig-Meyers furniture store across from Winn-Dixie, where his brother-in-law Wallace Tucker worked, to buy furniture for his new place. David had taken a bedroom set from the Toney Road house, but needed a dinette for his apartment.

David told Wallace he planned to fix a nice room for his sons. He set up a bed for Michael and a crib for Alex, and filled it with toys.

On September 21, 1994, Susan's attorney, Thomas White, served David with legal papers, asking for the divorce on the grounds of adultery. The complaint read, "During the course of this marriage, Defendant has carried on, and continues to carry on an adulterous relationship with a paramour known to plaintiff; due to this behavior and other irreconcilable differences, the parties herein separated . . . and have continued to live apart."

Susan was given sole custody of Michael and Alexander, with David receiving liberal visitation as long as he gave Susan forty-eight hours notice. Previously, Susan had complained that David had a habit of simply showing up at the house, and she didn't like it.

David agreed to pay Susan $115.04 per week in child support and pay health insurance coverage for the children at a cost of $112.58 per month. The couple agreed to split the children's medical or dental expenses not covered by health insurance.

Susan and David had built no equity in the Toney Road house, but David agreed to give his interest in the home to Susan. In return, Susan was solely responsible for paying the $340 monthly mortgage. David also agreed to pay her attorney's fee of $290.

"David said he didn't mind paying because he wanted what was best for his kids," a friend of his said. "He knew that Susan would never hold him out from seeing the kids."

The separation appeared to be going smoothly. On weekends, David picked up the boys and took them to his apartment, where they colored or played with blocks. Sometimes, he drove them to Veterans Park and let them feed the ducks. Occasionally, he went to the Toney Road house and mowed the grass. Michael loved to sit on his lap as they went up and down the lawn on a riding mower.

A year before the breakup, Susan Smith took a job at Conso Products Company, a company that manufactures decorative trimmings. Conso employs 536 people in the city of Union.

Susan was hired at $6.25 an hour to be the assistant to the executive secretary for J. Carey Findlay, the president and CEO of the company. Susan's job kept her in touch with various merchants in town. She frequently called the local bed-and-breakfast, The Inn at Merridun, to set up reservations for out-of-town clients. She ordered flowers from Joyce florist for clients and picked up meals and booked travel arrangements for Findlay. Those in town who got to know her voice on the telephone say she was always soft-spoken and polite.

J. Carey Findlay, the former Charlotte managing partner for an accounting firm, bought Conso in 1986, along with a group of investors. Originally, they'd planned to revitalize the fledgling company for a quick resale, but Findlay became fascinated by the business, bought out his partners in 1988 and moved to Union.

He and his wife, Koni, bought a 50-acre estate about seven miles south of Conso.

In November 1993, Conso became Union County's first publicly owned corporation when it announced a public offering of its stock. By the end of the year, Findlay had bought or opened factories in London, Canada and Mexico, and reported export sales—nonexistent four years ago—of $5 million.

Susan enjoyed working for a powerful man in a prestigious company. Conso was exciting and the opportunities seemed boundless.

Something else happened at Conso: Susan Smith fell in love. Hard. The man she wanted was Tom Findlay, one of three sons of J. Carey Findlay.

Tom, twenty-seven, had grown up in Mountain Brook, an upscale suburb of Birmingham, Alabama. He'd graduated from Auburn College in 1990 and then moved to Union to head up the graphic arts department of Conso. He designed and made brochures for the company.

Tom was outgoing and popular, especially among the town's young women. The secretaries at his father's company referred to him as "The Catch."

"Most of the young women in town are interested in Tom," said one local. "He's the town's most eligible bachelor. When women get attached to him, they can't let go."

At some point during Susan and David's estrangement, Tom Findlay asked Susan on a date. Over the next few months, they frequently met for lunch, and took in several movies together. Susan visited him at his cottage on his father's estate and attended one of Tom's well-known hot-tub parties. During the summer of 1994, Tom and Susan also both went to Conso's executive party.

It seemed as if things might work out after all. By now, Susan and David appeared to have an amicable relationship. In early October they attended Union's Agricultural County Fair, in a lot across the street from Winn-Dixie. As they strolled by the various exhibits David carried Alex, and Susan held Michael's hand. They bought lunch for the boys and chatted easily. That Sunday, the four of them went to church together.

But Susan's dream of stability and love still eluded her. While Tom Findlay liked Susan Smith, he swiftly began to feel that she was too possessive, too needy. As quickly as it had begun, the relationship was over.

On October 18, Tom Findlay typed out a letter to Susan on his computer. In it, he told her that she was a great person and had a lot going for her. He encouraged her to continue her college education, and said he knew that someday she'd meet Mr. Right. Tom explained to her that he was not her Mr. Right because he wasn't mature enough or responsible enough to take care of a wife and two children.

At the end, Tom Findlay told Susan that some guy would come along someday and make her happy.

Susan received the letter four days after her divorce papers were filed in court. She was furious, and let him know it. Tom was taken aback. Sweet, soft-spoken Susan? Tom Findlay knew for sure he'd made the right decision.

As for Susan, the rejections were mounting.

On October 24, a Monday night, Susan picked up her children from the Cathcarts and brought them to the home of her best friend, Donna Garner. Donna's parents baby-sat while Susan met with a professor at the University of South Carolina in Union. Around 7:30, she and Donna stopped in at the only bar in Union, Hickory Nuts. The bar had opened four months earlier, and was a popular meeting spot for the town's young people. They played pool and ate chicken wings. On weekends, they would sing along with a karaoke machine.

That night, when Susan and Donna arrived, Tom Findlay was already seated at the bar, talking to two married women whom he had known for some time. One, in fact, was the wife of a good friend, a young man they were waiting for. Tom was well known at Hickory Nuts, stopping in after work two or three times a week.

Susan and Donna Garner took seats a few stools away from Tom and his friends and Susan ordered a beer. Still stung by their angry words of the previous week, Tom and Susan did not speak.

When the bartender tallied up the tab, Tom told her to put Susan and Donna's drinks on his bill. Susan said nothing to him when she left, about half an hour later.

That night, when Susan picked up her sons, Donna Garner's parents remembered how she dropped to her knees and played with little Alex, kissing and hugging him.

The next day, Tuesday, October 25, Susan joined a staff of nine from Conso at lunch at Andy's in Buffalo. The group sat in the back room, pushing two tables together. Tom Findlay had a turkey club platter and unsweetened iced tea; Susan ordered the grilled Italian chicken dinner, baked potato, steamed vegetables, and water.

Although Tom and Susan sat next to each other, Susan was noticeably quiet throughout the meal and ate little. "Everyone was laughing and talking," the waitress recalled, "but Susan wasn't."

When lunch was over, Susan paid the $50 bill with a company check, leaving an $8 tip.

She returned to work shortly after one P.M., but by 3:30 she told a supervisor that she needed to leave early. She was near tears.

"She seemed very upset," the supervisor said later. "I asked if she wanted to talk about it and she said no, but maybe later."

Susan left Conso and walked to the parking lot. She climbed in the Mazda Protege and drove to pick up her sons. When Michael and Alex left the playroom for the last time, they waved goodbye to their baby-sitter Judy Cathcart and to the other children.

"See you tomorrow," someone said.

6

Most Union residents heard the news about the carjacking from William Christopher, the news director at Union's only radio station, WBCU 1460 on the AM dial. The slim, deep-voiced thirty-five-year-old Carlisle resident had left his home around five A.M. that Wednesday, October 26, driving the ten miles to Union.

He had heard a mention of a carjacking on the 11:00 P.M. local news the night before. Knowing that such an unlikely crime in peaceful Union would be the day's big story, he left a little early for work. On his way to the station he stopped in at the Union city police station just before 5:30 for the latest news.

The officer on duty gave him an update: Sheriff Wells and his deputies had called in the South Carolina Highway Patrol and officials from SLED. Dozens of men were searching the woods and area around John D. Long Lake, near the stretch of Highway 49 where Susan Smith said the carjacker had commandeered her Mazda.

Before he left, Christopher picked up a composite drawing of the suspect. A police artist had met with Susan in the early morning hours and, using the description she provided, sketched out a rough draft of what the man looked like. Susan had described him as a black man, around forty years old, wearing a dark cap, a dark shirt, jeans, and a plaid jacket.

Christopher arrived at WBCU's offices just before the start of his 6:00 A.M. shift. Settling into his chair in the station's control booth, he told Union's early risers that a Union resident had been the victim of a carjacking on Highway 49 and that the woman's two young sons had been taken along with the car. Police were conducting a huge manhunt in the area, he said, and he encouraged residents to stop by the station to pick up a flyer with a composite of the suspect. By mid-morning he'd handed out dozens of flyers.

One of his listeners that morning was Dot Frost, Susan's neighbor. She had gotten up early to pick up her granddaughter from her daughter's house down the block. Her daughter, who also worked at Conso, was going on a business trip to Hickory, North Carolina and Dot was to care for the child for a few hours in the morning until it was time to drop her at the baby-sitter's.

Dot's daughter met her at the door. "Momma, that carjacking at Monarch? That's Susan," she said. "It's Susan's two little boys."

Dot immediately thought of the outside light at Susan's house, still dark. "I knew something was wrong," she told her daughter. "Always. She always leaves the light on." Dot Frost thought of little Michael sitting on his dad's lap as he rode the lawn mower, and Alex, the baby, how he always smiled.

Dot began to cry.

On the other side of Union, Carlisle Henderson, seventy-one, was also tuned in to William Christopher's broadcast. Henderson, too, worked for WBCU. For the last eight years, he'd been hosting his own weekday and Sunday morning show, *Carlisle Henderson's Gospel Hour*, playing Christian music and leading listener prayers.

As he heard about the carjacking and Susan Smith's missing boys, Carlisle called to his wife, Georgia, to come and listen. The couple took in the news in amazement. Their granddaughter, Jennifer, was a good friend of both Susan and David, and Georgia Henderson had grown up with Linda Russell's mother, Eulala, Susan's grandmother. Their son, Tommy, had once worked for Bev Russell at the appliance store.

Now and then, Carlisle bumped into Susan and the children at Wal-Mart or Winn-Dixie.

"Boy, you're just as beautiful as your mother," Carlisle would say, then add teasingly, "And these kids! Why, I'm going to take those kids and run with them." He remembered how Susan would laugh. *A sweet, sweet young lady,* he always thought.

Later that morning, as *Carlisle Henderson's Gospel Hour* went on the air, the three phone lines at WBCU lit up continuously. One by one, Union residents called in to ask for prayers for Michael and Alex Smith.

That, in the face of tragedy, the people of Union should turn to God and each other is hardly surprising. If ever there was a community built on faith and fellowship it is this tiny hamlet tucked in the foothills of the Blue Ridge Mountains in the Piedmont section of upstate South Carolina.

The city and county of Union got its name from the old Union Church that stood not far from Monarch Mill, the spot where Susan claimed to have been carjacked. In its early days, the town was known as Unionville; later it was shortened to Union. The Union Church was home to three denominations: Methodist, Baptist, and Presbyterian, all of whom worshiped together at the same services.

The first white settlers came to Union from

Virginia in 1749, settling down between the Pacolet and Tyger rivers and at Fairforest Creek. But the years between 1763 and the start of the Revolutionary War saw the greatest migration into Union County. Settlers built log cabins and planted tobacco, flax, corn, and wheat in the area's fertile soil.

Union was one of the first towns settled in the area and one of the few that escaped the bloody ravages of the Civil War. It stood untouched during Union General William Tecumseh Sherman's bloody march to the sea because the Broad River flooded and turned the troops away, leaving intact the town's more than two dozen stately antebellum homes. Some of them, including the Inn at Merridun on the outskirts of downtown, are now open to the public as bed-and-breakfast establishments.

Union County has a population of 30,337; the city of Union, the largest municipality, has a population of 9,836. Of those, 69.8 percent are white and 29.9 percent are black.

Union County also includes several smaller communities including Jonesville, Whitmire, Pacolet, Lockhart, Carlisle, and Buffalo. The towns are home to many industrial and manufacturing plants providing employment to 13,180 people. A large portion of the county has been reserved as part of Sumter National Forest.

The city of Union is known as "The City of Hospitality." Signs boast the friendliness of its residents. On the water tower in town is a painted image of two hands clasped in a handshake. "Hospitality a Tradition. People make a difference." And the community has also been known for its patriotism. In the early days of World War I, Union County won nationwide acclaim as the only county in the United States that did not have a military draft—because its draft quotas were filled by volunteers.

Per capita income in the city of Union is $9,231; the median family income, $25,762, and median household income, $18,794. Union has a downtown district, four shopping centers, and a campus of the University of South Carolina. It also boasts South Carolina's first Carnegie Library and several historic public buildings and districts, including its 1823 jail, which is no longer used. It was designed by Robert Mills, a South Carolina native known for designing the Washington Monument.

Across from the old jail is the headquarters of the Union County Sheriff's department, where in the early morning of October 26, the day after the alleged carjacking, a massive manhunt was getting underway. At 8:00 A.M., the phone rang in Howard Wells's office. He picked it up on the first ring.

"Sheriff Wells," he said.

It was his wife, Wanda. She knew to make it quick. "I know you're probably busy, but I just want to know if you need anything or I can do anything for you," she said.

"No," he said. "I'm fine."

"Okay." A concerned Wanda hung up. She wondered if her husband had had anything to eat. Probably not. She knew when he was upset or involved in a case he wouldn't eat or sleep. She never pushed him. It wouldn't make any difference anyway.

Wanda drove to Union Federal Savings Bank, where she'd worked for nineteen years. In recent years she'd been promoted to assistant vice president and director of human resources and was given a small office in the back. As she walked in and said good morning to her co-workers, she heard them talking about Susan Smith and the carjacking.

Suddenly the name rang a bell. Wanda remembered seeing Susan and the children at Scotty and Wendy Vaughan's house, and also on occasion at the bank, where Susan had an account. Wanda Wells suddenly realized who Susan Smith was.

She's Wendy's sister-in-law, she thought.

Across the street Wanda's husband was working the phones. Gathering the manpower was critical at the start of an investigation. He handed his secretary, Michelle Peahuff, his scribbled notes from his late-night interview with Susan Smith and asked her to type it up as soon as possible. He knew the media would be asking for the copy of the report.

When she was done, he reviewed it quickly. Atop the report, in the section labeled "Comments," the dispatcher had written: "Caller stated there was a hysterical woman telling him a man jumped in her car at red light and took her children & car. 1990 Mazda Protege, burgundy in color, SC TAG GBK 167."

Under "Complaintant," Wells listed Shirley McCloud.

In the section marked "Victims," was written:

Susan V. Smith, 23, ht. 5ft. 3, 130 lbs, brown hair, brown eyes.

Michael D. Smith, 3, 3ft tall, 30 lbs. brown hair, brown eyes.

Alexander Smith, 1, 2ft. 4 inches, 25 lbs. Hair, blonde, eyes, brown.

407 Toney Road.

The Mazda Protege was listed as stolen, with a value of $6,500.

On the second page of the report, under "Narrative," Wells described the events Susan had related to him: "The victim in this case states that a black man armed with a handgun entered her vehicle on Highway 49 while she was stopped at the stoplight at the intersection of Monarch Highway. He told her to drive northeast on Highway 49, just below the John D.

Long Lake. He told her to stop, and then ordered her to exit the vehicle at gunpoint. When she asked him about getting her children out, the subject said, 'I don't have time, I won't hurt them,' and then the subject proceeded northeast on Highway 49. Suspect, a black man was wearing a dark-colored toboggan cap, a plaid jacket, red with blue or navy, blue jeans, and a dark-colored shirt under the jacket. All Union County deputy sheriffs were notified immediately to begin searching. The South Carolina Highway Patrol was notified and sent four men. SLED was notified and sent fourteen men and a helicopter."

That afternoon, Wells asked SLED agents to take a statement from Shirley and Rick Mc-Cloud. The agents showed up at the McCloud home shortly after the family returned from work. They asked questions about Susan's arrival the previous night, and about what she had told them before Sheriff Wells arrived.

"Do you remember what she was wearing?" a SLED agent asked.

Rick Jr. said he did. "Light blue jeans, white tennis shoes, white socks, a white T-shirt, and a white sweatshirt with orange letters."

"Do you remember what it had written on it?"

He thought a moment. "Clemson."

"You sure about that?"

Rick Jr. nodded. "Ninety-nine percent sure. It's Clemson."

"You sure? What about Auburn?"

Rick Jr. shook his head. "Clemson."

The SLED agent hid a smile. The university named on Susan's sweatshirt had been Auburn.

That afternoon, Margaret Frierson was at her desk at the Adam Walsh Center, an organization for missing children, in Columbia, South Carolina, about seventy miles south of Union, when a reporter from Channel 4 in Greenville phoned.

"What are the statistics of carjackings involving children?" the reporter asked.

Margaret told the reporter that he should call Hugh Munn, the public information director of SLED. She gave him the number, and then quickly called Munn herself. She usually liked to warn Munn when he should expect a call from the media. As the phone rang, Margaret wondered about the reporter's request. What was going on?

It was Munn who told Margaret about the carjacking and the disappearance of Michael and Alex Smith. He said that she would likely be getting a call from the family very soon.

A short time later, she did. Wendy Vaughan, Susan's sister-in-law, sounded hesitant on the phone, unsure of what she wanted.

"I know I need to call you," she began. "We need some help."

Margaret knew the stress involved in missing children cases. The South Carolina office of the Adam Walsh Center was one of four such organizations that grew out of the July 1981 disappearance of six-year-old Adam Walsh from a Florida department store.

Adam had gone to a Sears store in Hollywood, Florida with his mother, Reve to return an item. As they passed the electronics department, Adam pleaded with his mother to allow him to stay and play with an Atari video game while she went to the sales counter. At first Reve Walsh said no, it wasn't safe, but Adam promised he wouldn't stray and his mother finally gave in. Reve was away just three minutes. When she returned, her son was gone.

Adam Walsh was missing for ten days. His disappearance sparked an intense hunt. His mutilated body was discovered 150 miles southwest of Hollywood. Police believe he had been tortured.

Back then, there was no blueprint for law enforcement to follow. No computer lists of suspected child molesters, no clearinghouse for missing children, no way for one law enforcement agency to know what another was doing. His killer was never found.

Spurred on by their grief, Adam's parents lobbied to change that. In 1984, in large part due to their efforts, Congress passed the Missing Children's Act, which organized a computerized system for sharing information and established four regional missing children centers, in Columbia, Ft. Lauderdale, New York and Los Angeles. Their function is to help get the word out when a child is reported missing and to help support the family throughout the crisis. The first Adam Walsh Center opened in Fort Lauderdale in honor of the child whose murder sparked extraordinary change in federal laws.

Margaret tried to put Wendy at ease. "Are you calling about the two small children in Union?" she asked. "I can take preliminary information from you, but I would need to speak to one of the parents."

Wendy explained that Susan and David were with Sheriff Wells at the moment but she promised to get a message to them. "I'll have someone call you back," she said.

But Susan and David remained tied up with the police investigation, and eventually, it was Beverly Russell who called Margaret back. The two talked for a few minutes, and Margaret told Beverly that she and her assistant, Charlotte Foster, would be in Union the next day. Beverly Russell gave Margaret the directions to his home, and thanked her for her help. That night, Margaret and Charlotte stayed in the center's office until almost eight arranging with SLED to pick up photos of Michael and Alex.

They would be coordinating the printing of

thousands of flyers bearing the boys' photos. It was their job to make sure the public knew of two little South Carolina boys whose parents wanted them home.

It was almost nine that Wednesday night when Sheriff Howard Wells pulled into the driveway of his home on Toney Road. He'd been gone for thirty-six hours.

Wanda met him at the door.

"Have you had anything to eat?" she asked.

"Very little," Wells replied.

"Do you want anything?"

Wells shook his head.

"No, I don't want anything," he said. "I'm just going to take a shower, and shave and change clothes and go back to work."

Wanda looked at her husband's worn face. "Howard, you need to get some rest," she said gently.

Wells turned and looked directly at his wife. "No," he said firmly. "I need to find the children."

Wanda Wells did not reply. She knew not to say more. The sheriff headed toward the back of the house and a minute later, Wanda heard the water running. Half an hour later, he was gone.

7

Every morning, before they left for work, Shirley and Rick McCloud stood by their den window, looking out at Highway 49. It had become their ritual ever since Susan Smith arrived at their door.

They'd stare out at the road and the trees by the turnoff to John D. Long Lake. And Shirley would say the same words, again and again.

"Where are those kids? Where are those kids?"

Her husband would put his arm around her. He had no answer.

On Thursday morning, two days after Susan's story of the carjacking, Shirley woke before dawn and felt a growing sense of dread. The house was frigid, the winds outside blowing harder, stronger than they had since last winter.

She turned to her husband, near tears. "It's

so cold, Rick," she said. "Oh, God, those kids. I hope whoever has got them is taking care of them. I hope they're okay."

A few miles away, the Russell household was teeming with activity. Susan and David had been staying with Bev and Linda Russell since the night of their sons' disappearance. The three-bedroom house was always jammed with people. David's father, Charles David Smith, and his wife, Susan, flew in from California. David's uncle Doug and his wife arrived from Michigan. There were friends and cousins, ministers and neighbors. They slept on couches and in sleeping bags. Usually, the family slept in shifts, giving everyone a chance to get some rest.

When the house became too jammed, friends and family spilled into the screened-in porch off the den. In the evenings, when the reporters had left their posts in the driveway, the family gathered in the carport, greeting visitors as they came up the walk.

Church members and neighbors brought over enormous home-cooked meals to bolster the family as they kept up their vigil for the missing boys. Every day, Scotty Vaughan stopped in at a local restaurant and picked up a donated cooler of ice for sodas and juice.

The families of Susan and David Smith tried to comfort each other, offering a shoulder, an encouraging word, prayers. Every day, someone in the group would repeat the words that had become their mantra in the days since the disappearance: stay hopeful, stay positive, and pray.

Susan, it seemed, never spent a moment alone. Always, friends and family surrounded her. It was an odd change—the loneliness of her past was suddenly replaced by absolute love and support. Perhaps the horror of what she did was somehow muted in this atmosphere of sympathy and caring.

David, though, reacted differently, wanting more often to be alone. He would slip into a back bedroom at the Russell home and close the door. The families respected his privacy.

"You could tell when it got to him," a friend said.

Two days after the alleged carjacking, Margaret Frierson and Charlotte Foster from the Adam Welsh Center arrived at the Russell house. Susan and David had been told the women had worked with other families to find their missing children, but they didn't know what to expect.

There were so many people in the house, they retired to a back bedroom to talk alone. Ordinarily, the women prefer to speak primarily to the parents of the children, but because the family was so close, they agreed to meet with Susan, David, Bev, Linda, and Scotty Vaughan.

For forty minutes, Margaret told the group about the center and what it does to help the parents of missing children. She explained that she and Charlotte could be the family's liaisons with the news media, arranging interviews and broadcasting pictures of the missing children and information about the crime. They would help arrange to have flyers printed up with photos of the boys and a police department sketch of the suspect, and would see that they were sent to missing-children centers throughout the nation. At those centers, volunteers would distribute the flyers, blanketing their areas with information about the crime. If a video of the children were available, the women said, they would help produce a public service announcement and arrange to have it broadcast on national and cable television. They could also field offers from people who wanted to set up rewards for information leading to the return of the children.

The family seemed overwhelmed by the women's offer of assistance. Though Margaret and Charlotte had much more to talk to them about, Susan and David had to cut the conversation short.

They were needed at the sheriff's office. Charlotte stayed behind at the Russell house, answering the phone, and Margaret followed the young Smith couple in her car. In the six years she had been executive director of the South Carolina Chapter of the Adam Walsh Center, Margaret had worked with most of the sheriffs in the state's forty-six counties. But Wells was relatively new on the job in Union County, and there hadn't before been a missing child case under his watch. Margaret knew it was important to advise the sheriff early on of the center's capabilities. Every bit of help might lead to the safe return of Michael and Alex.

Outside Wells's office, the throng of reporters and camera crews was thick. They had begun arriving the day before, and by Thursday, the motels in town were booked solid. Satellite trucks lined Main Street. As Wells questioned Susan in his office, Margaret and SLED's Eddie Harris, a tall man with a neatly trimmed mustache, talked to David about making a plea for the safe return of the children on national television. Both Margaret and Harris believed that a nationally televised appeal could be instrumental in solving the boys' disappearance. But they both made one thing clear: David needed to make his own decision on what he planned to say.

"You say what you're comfortable with, don't try to say something because we tell you to say it," Margaret told him. "Speak from the heart."

Margaret reassured him that he didn't need to worry about fending off questions from the media. "You don't have to answer any questions if you don't want to," she said.

David nodded and swallowed hard. He was a little nervous, but he felt ready. He knew it was important to reach the greatest number of people. He wanted his boys back so badly, he would do anything to help find them.

Margaret slipped outside and quickly counted the number of microphones and cameras. She figured it might help David to know what to expect.

Wearing a blue sweatshirt and jeans, a solemn-looking David Smith met with the press for the first time on the steps of the Union County Sheriff's Department.

"To whoever has our boys, we ask that you please don't hurt them and bring them back. We love them very much . . . I plead to the guy to please return our children to us safe and unharmed. Everywhere I look, I see their play toys and pictures. They are both wonderful children. I don't know how else to put it. And I can't imagine life without them."

When he finished his appeal, David was escorted back inside the sheriff's office and Eddie Harris turned to Margaret.

"I think they want to hear something from you," he said.

Margaret hesitated for just a moment. She was acquainted with most of the local reporters and camera crews but she wasn't used to such national exposure. Still, she knew how important it was to speak out and talk about the Adam Walsh Center and its functions. And she too took her place before the cameras.

It was the first step in what would become a massive media campaign to find the boys. Over the next twenty-four hours, Margaret Frierson and Charlotte Foster would work with WIS, a local Columbia NBC affiliate, to produce a thirty-second public-service announcement about the missing children. The evening before, Linda Russell had given them a video she had taken at little Alex's first birthday party seven weeks earlier. On the tape, the boys played together and laughed. Susan was seen helping Alex unwrap his presents.

Margaret wrote the script and had a WIS staffer supply the voice-over. She made sure it was supplied to all of NBC's stations and cable affiliates around the country. She sent photos and flyers in overnight mail packets to dozens of missing children centers, including the three other Adam Walsh groups and the Polly Klaas Foundation in Petaluma, California. She called paper companies to persuade them to donate paper to Union businessman Mike Stevens, the owner of Stevens Printing Company on Highway 176. The day after the boys disappeared, Stevens had put all his orders on hold and devoted his presses to printing up more than 50,000 flyers with pictures of the Smith boys at no cost to the town or the family.

The hours were arduous, the pressure intense. For the next week, Margaret and Charlotte were in Union every day, camped out at the dining room table in the Russell home. Charlotte often manned the phones, taking dozens of messages from well-wishers and reporters, while Margaret continued to spread word of the boys' disappearance. It was exhausting work, but the two women were dedicated to their cause. They had to be. The lives of children were at stake.

Inside the office of Sheriff Howard Wells, the investigation was continuing at top speed. Early Thursday morning, Wells appeared on the *Today* show and later in the day, on *Larry King Live*. "We are going to look at everything and rule out nothing until we can do it with evidence," he said, on *Today*. He told the nation that his office had received more than 1,000 calls but so far they had no strong leads to follow. "Very rarely do you have a crime and not have a crime scene to work," he told the press. "I've been in law enforcement twenty years and I've never had a case where there is so little to work on."

Meanwhile, divers divided their time between searching a canal in Lockhart and scouring the bottom of John D. Long Lake. They spent hours in the murky waters but found nothing. Experts had made a considerable error: they assumed that anyone trying to get rid of a car would drive it into the water fast. No one considered that the driver of the Mazda would let it simply roll from the edge of the banks. Although it would be easy to imagine that a car driven into a body of water at high speed would go out further than a car driven slowly, in reality, the opposite is true. The faster the car hits the water, the more waves it creates, stopping the forward momentum. A car driven fast into a lake would simply drop and sink right there at the edge. But the Mazda had simply rolled into the water, and, as a result, had drifted out much further than anyone anticipated, nearly 100 feet. While the divers searched the edges of the lake, the Mazda remained hidden from their view in the murky waters, the dreadful resting place for the bodies of Susan and David Smith's children.

Two days after the alleged carjacking, investigators were presented with an important development in the mystery of what had happened to Michael and Alex Smith: both David and Susan Smith submitted to polygraph tests administered by the FBI. David's test showed no signs that he knew anything about the disappearance of his sons. But Susan's test proved inconclusive. One thing was certain: she showed the greatest level of deception when asked the question: "Do you know where your children are?"

The investigators did not hide the test results from Susan. Concerned, Susan told David that she thought she had not done well on the test. She wasn't sure she'd failed, she told him, but she said she thought perhaps the police were beginning to doubt her story.

Susan didn't have to ask David if he believed her. He did.

But Wells and the other agents were far more skeptical. Investigators confronted Susan with the discrepancies in her story. On Tuesday night, when she was near hysterics, she had told Wells about the red light, and how the black man jumped in the car. There had been no one around, Susan said. Not a single car on the road.

But the investigators knew differently. The light at the Monarch intersection is permanently green unless a car on the cross street triggers the signal to switch. If there had been no other cars around, the light would not have been red.

And there was another inconsistency. When asked where she had been heading when she was carjacked, Susan said she was on her way to visit Mitchell Sinclair, the fiancé of her best friend, Donna Garner. Mitchell lived less than a mile north of the Monarch intersection, in a rambling old house left to him by his grand-mother.

But, Susan was told gently, investigators had spoken to Mitchell, and he hadn't been expecting her. In fact, it was unlikely he had been expecting anyone. The house, investigators discovered, was a mess. Besides, that Tuesday at 9:00 P.M., Mitchell wasn't even home.

Something else was nagging at the men interrogating Susan. Where was she in the hours before nine? Susan had the answer ready—she'd taken the children shopping at Wal-Mart. They'd strolled through the store for quite a while, actually.

But a short time later, that story collapsed. SLED agents told Susan that investigators had canvassed Wal-Mart, talking to many people who were working or shopping that night. No one remembered seeing her or her two little boys.

Susan thought a moment, and then responded. She wasn't really at Wal-Mart, she explained. She'd actually just been driving for hours with the boys in the back seat. She hadn't said anything earlier, she told them, because she was afraid it might sound suspicious.

The investigators listened with growing concerns. By now, Sheriff Wells was heading up the investigation searching for the car and the children and meeting daily with the SLED team. The interrogation of Susan Smith had been taken over by behavioral specialist David Caldwell and investigator Lansing "Pete" Logan, both seasoned SLED agents.

But Howard Wells knew he needed to continue a parallel investigation into Susan Smith. It was simply good police work. The summer before Susan Smith made headlines, Wells had gone to the FBI's National Academy at Quantico, Virginia, earning fifteen college credits and finishing first in his class. He also attended the National Sheriffs Institute's Executive Development Program. He was elected class president and finished at the top of the class.

Although at times it seemed the entire nation was searching for Michael and Alex Smith Wells's investigation was proving frustrating. A Salisbury, North Carolina, convenience store was robbed by a black man in a car with South Carolina plates, but no children were seen in the car. By Friday morning, a Maryland fugitive had been arrested.

Later, about 200 people combed the Uwharrie National Forest in Rowan, Davidson, Stanly, and Montgomery counties in North Carolina after a deer hunter reported hearing a child's cries. Nothing was found.

The sheriff's instincts were sharp. But even as he continued to wade through tips and leads flowing through his office, Howard Wells suspected that the greatest source of information on the whereabouts of Michael and Alex Smith was the pretty young woman seated in his office.

As sure as Wells was that Susan had information she wasn't revealing, David Smith was certain his wife was the victim. He became annoyed that the sheriff's department continuously asked Susan to meet with investigators. He couldn't understand why they were wasting precious time talking to Susan. She'd said all she knew.

David couldn't stop thinking about his boys. He kept replaying his last Sunday visit with Michael and Alex. He'd seen them for seven hours that day. They hadn't gone anywhere, they'd just stayed in his apartment and played. He'd gotten some wooden blocks and he and Michael had stacked them higher and higher, and then Alex would toddle over and knock them down. How they laughed, his Alex and Michael.

When Susan had arrived to pick up the children, David had hugged and kissed his sons good-bye. At the last minute he had decided to walk them all down to Susan's car.

That was the last time he saw them, as they drove away in the back seat of their mother's Mazda Protege.

[8]

The doubts about Susan's story hit the front page of the *Union Daily Times* on Saturday, October 29. Quoting unnamed sources, the paper reported that Susan's lie detector test had raised the possibility that she was not telling the truth about the disappearance of her children. The story pointed out that Mitchell Sinclair had not been expecting Susan the night of the carjacking, that no one had seen her at Wal-Mart and that she now maintained she had been driving aimlessly in the hours before she was carjacked.

In some ways, the front-page report merely echoed the doubts many already harbored but hesitated to express. Some who had spoken to Susan in the days following the alleged carjacking had been disturbed by her odd demeanor. One woman who knew Susan well called several times to offer her prayers. Each time, after they talked for a few minutes, Susan would end the conversation saying, "I'll always cherish the memories of my babies."

Susan's reluctance to speak publicly to raise awareness of the missing children fueled talk that something was amiss. On the few occasions Susan did appear on camera to talk about the carjacking, many who knew her felt something was wrong.

During one of her early television appearances, Susan told how the carjacker had pushed her out of the car. She recalled her last words to Michael. "He said, 'Mama, where are you going?' and I told him, 'Baby, I've got to go, but you're going to be okay.'" She said she had yelled, "I love y'all," to her sons, as the Mazda sped off. "I just feel hopeless," she told reporters, sniffling. "I can't do enough. My children wanted me. They needed me. And now I can't help them. I just feel like such a failure."

Dot Frost was one of the early skeptics of Susan's story. The Smiths' neighbor knew what it was like to lose two boys. Once, Dot Frost had had four children, three boys and a daughter. Their school pictures lined the walls of her living room, dozens of photos of all four, at all ages.

Joey died first. It was Mother's Day, 1974. He was twenty-seven. Joey had just had surgery on his shoulder to remove a cancerous mole. He had bought a boat and gone fishing with friends in Lake Murray near Columbia. When they returned to the shore, the boat drifted away, and Joey dove in to retrieve it. His shoulder ached, and he suddenly realized he didn't have enough strength in his arm to be able to swim or even hold on to the boat. He drowned just off the shore.

Two years later, Danny died of leukemia. He was just fifteen.

The ache in a mother's heart does not heal, Dot knows. And in the days after Susan Smith's little boys were supposed to have been kidnapped, Dot watched Susan's eyes. And she shook her head.

She doesn't shed tears like I did when I lost my boys, she thought. *The tears, they came down. These tears of Susan's . . . I have a feeling those are crocodile tears.*

There was more. Dot's son Scott told her he was sure he saw Susan's car pull out sometime between 8:15 and 8:30 the night of October 25. He said he was watching television and got up during a commercial. The front door of the house was open, and Scott noticed Susan's Mazda backing out of the driveway.

When Susan's early statements about going to Wal-Mart or driving for hours were reported in the local news media Scott Frost was taken aback.

"Ma, she couldn't have gone to Wal-Mart or

rode around," he had told his mother. "I saw her. No way."

The Frosts didn't advertise their suspicions, but when a SLED investigator who'd been camped out in front of Susan and David's house for three days, showed up one afternoon and asked about the last time they'd seen Susan, Dot told him about the porch light and what her son had seen.

The investigator jotted down what she said. As he left, he suggested she not discuss what they'd talked about to the press. "Best thing, don't talk to anybody," he said.

Dot shrugged. She didn't think her opinions were all that important, anyway. But she didn't like being told what to do with them.

She called after the investigator, "If I had my way, I'd open up that garage and search that house. You ain't done anything. You ain't even searched the house."

The investigator kept walking to his car. He didn't respond.

Later, when a local news reporter knocked at her door, Dot Frost decided she had every right to express her feelings. When he asked if she believed Susan, she told him the truth. "It's like fishy," she said. "It looks suspicious."

That night, Dot got an anonymous phone call. "I hope you rot in hell," the caller snapped, and slammed down the phone.

* * *

Susan's childhood friend, Stacey Hartley, also harbored doubts about Susan's story. She remembered how as a child Susan had sobbed when she lost her dog. Watching Susan on the news, Stacey was bewildered. *Something's not right,* she thought. *She's not telling the truth about something. She knows something.*

But what would be her motive? Stacey wondered. Susan knew she was going to have custody of the children. It wasn't as if there was a fight over it. Stacey came up with the only possibility that made sense. *Maybe she's doing this to get back at David,* she thought.

In any case, Stacey felt sure that the children were safe. *She just hid those kids somewhere,* she decided. *She's gotten somebody to keep those kids for her.*

After the Union paper broke the news of investigators' doubts, television reports began suggesting the carjacking story was a hoax as well. One night at the Russells', Susan watched a TV news broadcast and slammed her hand down on the side of an armchair. "How could they say I'd hurt my babies!" she snapped.

From early on, members of the media were clearly skeptical about Susan's story. Again and again, reporters implored the family for interviews. Those who had covered other cases of missing children were astonished by Susan's refusal to speak to the press. Most parents will do anything if they believe there is any chance at all it might help bring their children home.

Dozens of reporters camped out in front of the Russell home pouncing on anyone who walked in or out. Family members, friends, and ministers bore the brunt of the attention. Most ignored the microphones and the questions shouted as they hurried up the walkway.

As the family's liaison with the media, Margaret Frierson found herself bombarded by frustrated reporters as she traveled in and out of the Russell home.

"Why aren't they coming out of the house?" they asked her repeatedly. "Why won't they talk to us?"

Margaret refused to speculate.

"It's my role to be a child advocate. I'm not an investigator," she kept saying. "The investigators are doing their job. My job is to let America know that these two little boys are missing. I've stayed focused on that. We're not there to solve the crime."

But Frierson, too, was concerned. She firmly believed it would be beneficial for the Smiths to publicly speak out for their children and so she approached Margaret Gregory, the wife of David's cousin, whom the family had asked to serve as a spokesperson. Gregory met twice daily with Susan and David, discussing the various request for interviews. Now and then the family would issue a written statement but almost all requests for face-to-face interviews were turned down.

Gregory told Frierson that Susan was simply not up to talking to the press. Frierson suggested someone else go in her place. "If you all can't do it, how about another family member?" Margaret said. "I'll leave it up to you."

Despite her personal feelings, Margaret Frierson wanted the decision to be Susan's and David's. She knew from experience that missing children cases bring enough anxiety. If going in front of the media intensifies that anxiety, she won't ask a parent to do it. She knew she could continue to encourage the couple to talk, but with such enormous attention focused on the Russell home these days, Frierson decided the best route for her would be to continue to work through Margaret Gregory.

Even so, there were inevitable clashes between the anxious family and the media pursuing what had become one of the biggest stories of the year. Margaret Gregory demanded that reporters stay off the Russell property. When some got too aggressive, she often reminded them that no one was getting an exclusive. If they come out, she told them, everybody's going to get their chance. We're not going to show favoritism.

If anyone was a staunch supporter of Susan Smith, it was Shirley McCloud.

Ever since the night of October 25, reporters had hounded the McCloud family, stopping by the house at all hours, calling her at work, showing up on the grounds of Lockhart High School, where Rick Jr. taught grades nine through eleven. Early on, Shirley gave one interview, to a *Rock Hill Herald Journal* reporter. She had turned him down several times, but the reporter persisted and Shirley finally agreed. She set guidelines from the start; "I do not want to be misquoted," she told him firmly. "I do not. If you misquote me in any way, you will hear from me. Do not misquote me."

He didn't. Still, Shirley hoped the focus on her little house and her family would end. She did not want to be a part of this story. She wanted only one thing: for the sheriff's office to find those little boys and bring them home.

Shirley had seen the agony in Susan Smith that terrible night. She could still hear the young girl's tortured cries, how her entire body shook when she spoke. And so when the reports began to surface that investigators were doubting Susan's story, Shirley was angry.

That Saturday, four days after the alleged carjacking, Shirley spent the day with her sister, Iris, in Lockhart. They talked about Susan, as they had for days. Shirley's sister gingerly brought up a few sensitive issues.

Iris thought it strange that Susan never called to thank Shirley for her help that night.

"Don't you find that funny?" Iris asked.

Shirley did not. After all, Susan was distraught, she said. How could she think of thanking anyone for anything when her precious babies were missing?

When the suggestion was made that perhaps a family member might have made the call, Shirley dismissed it out of hand.

There was more. Iris was not convinced by Susan's television appearances.

"Something's just not right, Shirley," she said gently. "Something's just not right."

Shirley snapped at her sister. "I don't care. Iris, what do you want her to do? Sob and cry and wail and scream every time they interview her? Don't you think they've given her something to help her?"

When Shirley returned home from her sister's home around three P.M. Saturday, November 3, a network news team was parked in her driveway.

At first, Shirley told the reporter she was not interested. "I'm very private," she explained. "I don't want to be on TV."

But the young woman didn't give up. She pointed out that many people were now saying they did not believe Susan Smith's story. Now was an opportunity, she told Shirley, for her to speak out in Susan's defense.

Shirley mulled that over. If telling what happened that night and how she was reacting would help her, she thought, then she'd do that.

The brief spot turned into a five-minute segment on *Good Morning America* the following day. Joan Lunden asked Shirley point-blank if she believed Susan Smith.

Shirley was adamant: "Personally, I don't believe she had anything to do with it," she said.

And she meant it.

There was another issue surrounding the disappearance of Susan Smith's children: Susan's claim that the carjacker was a black man.

From the beginning, many in the black community found her story beyond credibility. A black man drives off with two white babies, and has somehow escaped a sighting? Word traveling through Union's black community was mostly skeptical.

That's how Gilliam Edwards felt. The fifty-three-year-old mill worker had grown up in Union. In recent months, he'd undergone neck surgery and spent several weeks out of work. With time on his hands, he'd read all the newspaper stories and watched all the broadcasts about the Smith story. He had no idea what happened to Susan Smith's children, but one thing he felt certain about: no black man was responsible for their disappearance.

He told his wife his feelings about Susan Smith's story. He argued about it with his older children. He talked about it on Main Street every day, where he is most comfortable.

"I do my talking in the street," he often says.

Gilliam stuck to his position. "No black person does something like that," he told whomever would listen. "We know we're ninety percent of the prison population, we been ninety percent since 1776. We know when we go down to that prison for certain crimes, we going to be taken care of. It ain't going to be tomorrow, it going be as soon as we get down there. One's bothering children, bothering old people, messing with the women. You going to get it, that's all. Any black guy would have to be completely out of his mind to commit such a crime. You see me? Big old black guy with two white kids? No, no."

Early on, Gilliam made up his mind that Susan Smith probably had the children hidden somewhere. "She carried those kids off," he told his frineds. "She gave 'em to the in-laws or something."

Still, it bothered him every time he saw the police sketch of the black man Susan claimed had stolen her sons. *It's embarrassing*, he thought. *People looking at you like that, people on the street. One of our people? No way. No way.*

[9]

It wasn't just Union's black community that was bothered by that composite of the alleged assailant. When cognitive graphic artist Jeanne Boylan first saw the crude image distributed by the SLED investigators she knew at once that if Susan Smith really had been carjacked a far more detailed drawing of the suspect would be key to apprehending a suspect.

For the past seventeen years, Jeanne has worked more than 7,000 cases, sketching the faces of child abductors and killers for law-enforcement officials around the country. In one of her most prominent cases, Jeanne sketched the drawing of Richard Allen Davis, the man ultimately accused of the kidnapping and murder of twelve-year-old Polly Klaas of Petaluma, California.

In the early weeks of Polly's abduction, detectives had met with Polly's two friends, also twelve years old, and produced a crudely drawn image of the man they said had walked into the house and carried Polly off.

The drawing was so unlike Davis that police who had encountered him the night of Polly's kidnapping insisted the man in the drawing could not be the man they saw. After Jeanne was called to help, she met with Polly's friends and sketched a strikingly detailed portrait of the young girl's abductor. When Richard Allen Davis was finally caught nine weeks after Polly disappeared, the accuracy of Jeanne's drawing was astounding.

In the past year, Jeanne stayed in touch with Polly's father, Marc Klaas. Since the murder of his only child Marc has given up his job as owner of a Hertz dealership in San Francisco to work full-time as an advocate for children. For a time, he served as a board member for the Polly Klaas Foundation, the child advocacy group organized in honor of his daughter.

Then, about a year after Polly's death, Marc formed his own organization, The Marc Klaas Foundation for Children, to lobby for stronger laws to protect kids and keep violent, repeat offenders behind bars. He also meets with families who are suffering through the disappearance of a child.

When the Susan Smith case broke, Marc and Jeanne teamed up again.

Marc learned of the case first. He got a call

from producers at the syndicated news magazine show *American Journal*. Previously, Marc had reported three stories on missing children for the program. Now, producers hoped he would go to Union and report on Susan Smith and her missing babies. They sent him newspaper articles about the case, and a copy of the composite of the suspect.

Marc agreed to go. He then suggested they bring Jeanne Boylan in as well.

"Jeanne will be able to put a face on the guy," he told them. "She can really help."

The *American Journal* producers were enthusiastic about Marc's suggestion, and Marc quickly put in a call to Jeanne. The forty-one-year-old Boylan had just returned from working on a case in Wisconsin in which a twelve-year-old girl, Cora Jones, had been murdered by a serial killer.

That Thursday afternoon, October 27, when Jeanne picked up the phone at her house in Bend, Oregon, Marc didn't waste any time.

"Jeanne, it's Marc. What are you doing right now?" he said.

Jeanne sighed. "Marc, I'm having one of the worst days of my life," she responded.

Marc barely heard her. "We've got a case," he said, his voice serious. He went on to tell Jeanne what he knew about Susan Smith and the carjacking. He told her the composite drawing done by SLED agents didn't look very promising.

Jeanne said she'd get back to him quickly. She quickly called the Columbia, South Carolina, office of the FBI. She found out the name of the head of the operation and faxed him a copy of her bio, listing the various cases she'd worked on.

Jeanne had worked with the FBI numerous times before and agents there were familiar with her work. But she was careful to follow protocol. She told the agent on the phone that she would not go to South Carolina without the FBI's knowledge and approval. She knew that despite her good intentions, it was important not to step on any toes.

In a few minutes, she had her answer: The FBI has been trying to contact *her*. Charlie Shepard, who handled press relations for Jim Oppy, the FBI Special Agent in Charge for South Carolina, had put in a call to the agency's San Francisco office, trying to locate Jeanne's phone number in Bend, Oregon.

Still, Shepard warned Jeanne Boylan that she might want to hold off coming to Union until police had checked out a lead from North Carolina. Reports had just surfaced that a black man driving a car with South Carolina plates had robbed a convenience store in North Carolina. Authorities were checking to see if there was any connection to the Smith carjacking.

"It might be premature," Shepard told

Jeanne. "We've got a lead we're working on. You might want to wait until morning."

Jeanne hesitated for a moment. She glanced at the clock. If she rushed, she might just make the last flight out of Redmond Airport, a 5:10 flight that connected to a red-eye from Portland to Charlotte, North Carolina. The airport was about thirty-five minutes from her home, and she needed to shower and pack.

"I think I can make that last flight," Jeanne said. "I'd rather be there, in case you're lead doesn't turn out to be anything." She hung up and hurried to pack. The phone rang again almost immediately.

"Are you going?" Marc Klaas asked her anxiously.

She told him she was. They agreed to meet at the Charlotte Airport. Her flight from Oregon got in at 7:15 A.M.; his, at 7:30 A.M.

When she arrived in Charlotte, Jeanne slipped into the ladies' room at the airport and changed into a Christian Dior black suit. It was her standard outfit for meeting with the FBI; she called it her "every-press-conference boring suit."

Jeanne hadn't quite worked out a good compromise on attire. She knew she had to present herself as a professional to the FBI agents; at the same time, in a crisis situation she always felt it was less threatening if she dressed more casually for the family.

When Marc's flight arrived, the two hugged at the gate. Jeanne worried about Marc—he looked exhausted. Dressed in an old purple sweatsuit, he had dark circles under his eyes. She knew what a difficult year it had been for him, first losing his daughter and then throwing himself on the front lines of the battle to keep repeat offenders behind bars, fighting politicians, other lobbies.

In recent months, he'd even found himself at odds with the other members of the board of directors of the Polly Klaas Foundation over his aggressive direction. As word of the internal squabbling had leaked out, Marc had taken a beating in the press. Some thought he was too much a showman, that perhaps his motives were less than genuine.

Jeanne knew differently. Seeing him at the gate, she felt a strong bond with him. She thought about how emotionally charged a missing-child case is, and how friendships that develop in the midst of one are so strong and so pure.

For the next hour and a half, as their chauffered towncar headed south to Union, Marc and Jeanne caught up on each other's lives. Jeanne told Marc about the Cora Jones case in Wisconsin and he listened sympathetically. It reminded Jeanne of the time when she and Marc learned of a twelve-year-old Midwestern girl who had been found murdered right around the time

Polly was taken from her home. Jeanne remembered how Marc had reacted, slamming his hand against the wall.

"Jesus Christ," he exploded. "Twelve years old is such a dangerous age in this country."

Marc told Jeanne about his campaign for a revised version of California's Three-Strikes-And-You're-Out law. He told her that he had originally backed the bill because he was led to believe it would put violent, three-time felons in jail for life. But, Marc told Jeanne, the bill signed by Governor Pete Wilson targeted three-time felons regardless of whether their crimes were violent or not.

It wasn't what was needed, Marc complained. It would only overflow the prison population and cost taxpayers astronomic sums.

As they approached Union, they began to discuss the Susan Smith case. By now, Jeanne had seen the composite drawing of the alleged suspect in the carjacking. She could hardly believe how crudely it would be drawn.

"The single most important thing is that image has got to be right," she told Marc, who nodded emphatically. "The investigators have limited resources. This composite looks as if it's somebody under a dim street light from fifty feet away. There's no detail at all. You could say this is a man sitting very passively as if he's on a Greyhound bus trip. No detail. It's a smudge with a hat on it."

Marc and Jeanne arrived in Union about 9:30 Friday morning. Satellite trucks were lined up in front of City Hall but only a few reporters lingered on the steps that early in the day.

Marc went inside to change out of his sweatsuit while Jeanne waited outside. She stood by the steps holding her art case and feeling uncomfortable. She worried that the cameraman would begin to question who she was. She knew that almost anything could be a story on a slow news day. Already word was out that a well-known artist was on her way to Union, and Jeanne didn't want anything to disrupt her chances of meeting with Susan Smith.

When Marc returned, they asked directions to the Russell house, where Susan was staying. When they arrived, they walked past surprised news crews and proceeded up the driveway.

They didn't get far. Margaret Gregory bounded out of the house and sternly told them to leave.

"Susan's not going to see you," she said, her voice flat. "She has no interest in seeing you."

Marc and Jeanne almost laughed. They tried to walk by Margaret. She stepped in front of them again.

"She's not going to see you," Margaret said, her eyes cold.

Jeanne couldn't understand it. In the more than 7,000 cases she'd worked she felt she had a sense of what was typical behavior and what wasn't. More than family, clergy, or counselors, a person in a situation like Susan Smith's would want to see a person who knows what she's going through. That person was Marc Klaas.

"Does she know who we are, and why we're here?" Marc asked.

"She's not seeing anyone right now," responded Margaret.

Jeanne pulled out some newspaper articles about her work sketching suspects and a copy of her resume. She included a copy of the *People* magazine cover story on Polly Klaas. In it, the story mentioned the accuracy of her sketch of Polly's killer.

"Please pass this to Susan," she said. "Marc is here to be a comfort to her and I'm here to put a face on this man and help get those children back."

Margaret Gregory took the papers wordlessly. Jeanne tried again.

"This really is a very, very gentle process," she said. "For most victims it's actually very cathartic to get that image out. It's like speaking a foreign language and getting someone who can understand you. To get this image down, a physical, tangible placement of that image."

Again, Margaret Gregory said nothing.

It's like talking to someone with no ears, Jeanne thought. *She says, "Susan's not seeing*

*anyone," no matter what you say, even if it's
not an appropriate response.*

As they left, Marc and Jeanne shared their
disbelief at their rejection at the Russell house.
Jeanne tried to give Margaret Gregory the benefit of the doubt.

"Maybe she really doesn't know," said Jeanne.
"We're presuming she's heard of Polly's case."

Still, it was very strange. "She's so unemo-
tional, so one-dimensional," she said.

"Like a little bulldog," added Marc. "She
doesn't understand. She does not get it."

They talked about Susan. They wondered if
Margaret Gregory would really relay their messages. Jeanne wondered if Susan was too fright-
ened to try to conjure up the image of the
carjacker again.

Marc thought about calling David Smith's
grandfather, James Martin, in California. He'd
spoken with him several days earlier, and Martin had seemed enthusiastic that Marc had
planned to make the trip to Union.

While Marc stayed behind at the Russell
house with the press, Jeanne headed back to
downtown and made her way to Sheriff Wells's
office. There she met Carol Allison, an FBI
agent. Jeanne was pleased to see that the bureau had a female agent on the case. When
Jeanne introduced herself, Allison said they had
been expecting her.

She showed Jeanne the faxes that had come

in to the sheriff's office from various citizens, stories about Jeanne Boylan and the work she did with victims.

Allison explained that they wanted to include Jeanne Boylan in a high-level meeting with the FBI agents, SLED, and Sheriff Wells, but first it needed to be cleared through the bureau's San Francisco office. As Jeanne waited she told Allison about her work.

As she spoke, Jeanne occasionally peered out from the small office where she sat with Allison and watched the chaos in the office of the sheriff. SLED agents in camoflouge walked in and out, half-eaten sandwiches lay strewn on desks. Four secretaries answered constantly ringing phones.

To almost every caller, they said the same words: "Thank you very much, but there's nothing we have for you to do."

Jeanne was amazed.

This is crazy, she thought. *In Polly's case, volunteers were so important.*

She figured SLED had its own methods for searching, but certainly there were things for volunteers to do—passing out flyers, sending mailings.

FBI Agent Allison interrupted her musings. She had just received the call authorizing them to include Jeanne Boylan in their strategy meeting. She motioned for Jeanne to follow her next door. Sheriff Wells was on the telephone. He looked up and nodded hello to Jeanne Boylan.

Moments later, nine FBI and SLED agents joined them. Allison closed the door to the sheriff's office.

"Now," said Allison. "Tell them what you told me."

Boylan told them about memory, and how a traumatized individual stores the image of a face. She told them how susceptible that image is to change. Now and then she glanced at Carol Allison, thinking, *Is this what you want?*

Apparently, it was. The law enforcement officials listened in rapt attention.

Jeanne explained her criticism of the original drawing of the suspect. "It's situationally inappropriate for a person entering a vehicle," she told them. "The positioning is wrong. He's void of emotion. There are a number of red flags in it. It's the drawing of someone very passive."

She talked about the Polly Klaas case, how early on detectives were frustrated by interviews with Polly's two friends, the only witnesses to her kidnapping. The two girls had seen the man for several minutes—he'd bound and gagged them, before grabbing Polly—but their descriptions of the kidnapper varied dramatically.

The differences were normal, Jeanne insisted. If they had been the same, that would have been odd.

She told them a little about how a traumatized mind digests an image, and about compulsive repetition, when the mind goes over and over the same event.

"Nothing impacts recall more than emotion," she said. "That's what happens under trauma. Your mind is trying to move that memory and gain mastery over it. The mind is so powerful it tries to protect you. It tries to feed new information into that memory that is more emotionally palatable."

At one point, Jeanne wondered if the FBI and SLED agents really understood her focus on memory, emotion, and perception. Those were very abstract terms, she knew, for men used to dealing with the details of police work.

She gave them an example about a murder weapon, a gun or a knife. If at first it has on it a single set of fingerprints, and then it is passed down through a dozen people, each holding it, touching it, by the time it is inspected, the weapon is covered with fingerprints, she said. It is no longer the same weapon it was at the beginning.

She explained that the traditional FBI method of analyzing an image from a victim's memory is much the same. The method, created in the 1940s, requires the victim to look through mug shots, a total of 960 full-facial photographs. The agents place little pieces of paper over various parts of the face—the mouth, nose, eyes.

"The actual image," Jeanne Boylan told them,

"begins to distort with exposure to as few as twelve photographs. It's an archaic method. And once that information is gone, it's gone."

SLED Chief Robert Stewart listened carefully. "Well, I don't think our person uses that technique," he said, reaching for the phone.

He called a subordinate and spoke for a few minutes. "They use the FBI Facial Identification Catalogue," he said.

Jeanne rolled her eyes, exasperated. That was just what she'd been talking about.

10

In the hour and a half Jeanne met with SLED investigators, FBI agents, and Sheriff Wells, she learned that the team investigating the Smith boys' disappearance did not believe Susan Smith at all.

At one point, a senior investigator asked a crucial question: "Do you have the ability to know if she is fabricating?"

Jeanne answered without missing a beat.

"I do," she said. "If you know what you're doing, you can really detect when someone is fabricating."

She would know very early on, she said, if Susan was providing actual information or merely making up details as she went along. "If you fabricate information it's very blatant," she said.

The men seemed excited by her words. One

said, "It's kind of a human lie detector test," and Jeanne nodded. They understood.

Later that day, Jeanne returned to the Russell home. She thought about what the law enforcement officials had said about Susan. Jeanne decided that she would make up her own mind about whether Susan was telling the truth. After all, Jeanne had been on many cases in the past where law enforcement were suspicious of the parents. She knew it was a part of their job to be a little distrustful of everyone.

Arriving at the house, Jeanne decided to distance herself from the reporters assembled along the road. She wondered if Susan could see her from the window, if Susan thought she was a reporter or an FBI agent.

By now, Jeanne had rented a car so she could come and go easily, and not depend on Marc Klaas and the team from *American Journal.* She had also decided to change her look, trading the stodgy black business suit for jeans and a shirt, and tucking her blond hair into a baseball cap.

But no matter what Jeanne did, Margaret Gregory always met her in the driveway with the words, "Susan's not interested."

Throughout the day, Jeanne checked in occasionally with the FBI. They told her that they couldn't force Susan to meet with her; if they did Susan would likely be hostile, which wouldn't help at all. Jeanne needed to be a neutral entity, someone Susan felt was on her side.

On the way back to the hotel, Jeanne and Marc shared their frustrations. They joked that they wished they could somehow tranquilize Margaret Gregory and slip by her. They were especially annoyed when they discovered that Margaret worked in public relations and was married to a cousin of David's. "A shirttail relative," they called her.

"It's so strange," Marc said. "It seems to me they are putting Susan ahead of the children's welfare. There's no time to waste. You have to find the children as fast as possible. They're making all the wrong moves."

Jeanne agreed. They headed to their rooms to get ready for dinner. Around 10:30 P.M., Jeanne used the hotel phone to check her messages at home in Bend. She listened in astonishment to a message left by a young woman about twenty minutes earlier.

"Jeanne, this is Tracy Wright," the young woman said with a thick Southern accent. "I'm taking media calls for Susan Smith. Susan is ready to work with you to develop a caricature of the abductor." Tracy left a number for Jeanne to call.

Jeanne grabbed a pen and jotted down the number. She hung up and ran down the hall. She pounded on Marc's door, ecstatic.

"Marc, she's going to meet with me!" she said, even before he opened the door.

She quickly explained about the message and the two friends devised a strategy. "I'll go in," Jeanne told him, "and once she meets me and understands I'm not a heavy-handed investigator, I'm a nice person to talk to, I'll try to get you in. If you're there, without cameras, by yourself, once I get in and have time with her, I think it will be okay."

They debated whether Jeanne should call the number Tracy had left right away, or wait until morning. "It might be too late to call now," Jeanne said, eyeing the clock. Marc agreed. They didn't want to do anything to upset the family. They were so close.

At dinner in the restaurant next door Marc and Jeanne felt relieved. That night, Jeanne could hardly sleep.

At 8:30 the next morning she called. A man answered, groggy from sleep.

Tracy, he grumbled, had gone to work. "I was just sleeping here in the bed," he said harshly.

When Jeanne explained who she was, the man gave her another number to call. When she did, Margaret Gregory answered the phone. It was her home number.

Jeanne sighed. This did not look good.

She tried. She told Margaret that a Tracy Wright had said Susan was ready to meet with her. Margaret's response didn't surprise her.

"Susan is not interested in doing this," Margaret said flatly.

Jeanne tried not to show her growing annoyance. "Well Margaret, I understand," she said. "But I got a call last night. I understand she is willing to see me."

There was silence on the phone.

"No," Margaret said. "Susan is not interested in doing this."

On the way to Union that morning, Jeanne and Marc talked it over again. "It sounds like Susan is wanting to work with you," Marc said. "Margaret hadn't even talked to her today, and she still said no."

"Well," said Jeanne, "If Susan is willing and Margaret is not letting me in, then Margaret's my enemy. I'm not leaving here until I make sure I know what Susan wants."

When she got to Union she drove directly to the Russells. She turned onto Mount Vernon Road and made the right turn on Heathwood Road, then she pulled right into the Russell driveway, driving almost to the end.

A group of relatives and friends of the Smiths and Russells looked out from the screened-in porch in astonishment. Just as Jeanne stepped out of the car, Margaret came running out of the house.

"We," she said icily, "are not interested in doing this."

Jeanne had had enough. "Okay," she said.

"That's fine. But I want you to understand there is going to be some public repercussion if she doesn't do this. The public is going to want to know why. There's going to be serious questions about this. I'm here to help put a face on the man who has these children. Do you understand?"

"Yes," Margaret said, "I understand."

At the same time, Marc, too, was trying his best to break down walls. On his first day in Union he had met briefly with Susan's stepfather, Beverly Russell, and Margaret Frierson from the Adam Walsh Center. Both thought it would be good for him to see Susan, but neither seemed to be able to arrange the encounter.

At one point, Marc and Jeanne considered the possibility that Susan and David Smith would not see them because of their relationship to *American Journal*. Perhaps, they wondered, they see us as reporters. Marc called producers at the show and told them if he got in to see the family, he wanted to do it privately, to give them the benefit of his expertise on searching for the children. The producers agreed.

Eventually, Marc left the Russell home and camped out in front of the Toney Road house, where David's father, Charles David Smith, his stepmother, Susan, and uncle, Doug, were staying. He got to know Dot Frost, and her husband, Earl. On Saturday night October 29, he spent a few hours sitting on their porch, talking about the case.

Just after eleven P.M., David Smith's Honda pulled into the driveway at the Toney Road house. Marc jumped up and ran across the street. David pulled out quickly and sped back down the street.

"That's it," Marc told Dot. "They don't want help. I'm going home."

He tried one more time. On Sunday, Marc managed to have a long talk with David's dad. Marc told him that he understood if Susan and David did not want to answer personal questions—all he wanted was to try and help them by offering what he'd learned about abducted kids. He'd been through it. He knew.

David's father was supportive. He was living in California during the nine weeks Polly Klaas was missing. He had seen Marc on television almost every night, pleading for help, criticizing the police investigation, demanding justice for his child.

"Get me in to see them," Marc said.

"I think it would be a good idea," David's father said slowly, his face drawn with pain.

He told Marc that he was so worried about the children, that nobody in the Russell home wanted to do anything or really fight for the kids. He agreed that the family should take advantage of the intense media coverage.

"I'll try very hard," he told Marc.

Then, David's father told him about his son Danny, and how it devastated the family when he died. Marc nodded. He understood the man's pain. Not an hour passed when he didn't think of his Polly.

The two men set a tentative appointment for 10:00 A.M. the following day. Marc would meet with Susan and David, but no cameras would be permitted.

By now, Jeanne had all but given up. On Sunday night, a reporter from NBC's *Dateline* television show interviewed Sheriff Wells about the possibility of a second drawing of the suspect. Wells told her there wasn't going to be one; he didn't want to confuse the public with another image.

When the reporter relayed this to Jeanne, she was stunned. She called Carol Allison and asked if the Sheriff had said that.

Allison came back sheepishly.

He had, she told Jeanne. "They asked him and he didn't know what else to say."

Jeanne sighed. She realized it had just been a careless remark made by the sheriff in the glare of the TV cameras, but she believed it had ended any chance she had for meeting with Susan. The only reason Susan might feel compelled to see her, she reasoned, is if she continued to feel intense pressure from the media. If Wells was saying that it was okay not to do a second drawing, Susan would certainly not bother with her.

Jeanne didn't blame Wells. He was under enough pressure already. But at this point, it seemed useless to stay in Union.

"I'm powerless now," Jeanne told Marc that night. "The sheriff accidentally took the wind out of my sails."

Marc said goodbye to Jeanne that night. She was catching a flight to New York. She had other work she'd been putting off for the past four days. Before she left, they talked about their belief that Susan knew where her children were. "At least if she is involved," Marc told Jeanne, "the kids are okay. She's probably got a relative that's got them stashed somewhere."

The next day, Marc showed up at the Russell house a few minutes early. He stopped and bought a bag of Danish pastries. Margaret Gregory met him in the driveway.

"They're not up to it right now," she said. "Maybe in a few hours."

Marc just looked at her. Then, Charles David Smith stepped out on the porch, upset.

"I thought it was all arranged," he told Marc, his eyes filling with tears. "I'm sorry. I'm sorry."

The older man sat on the stoop of the Russell house and began to cry. Marc didn't know what to say. He felt powerless. He couldn't help the family if he couldn't get in to see Susan and David.

David's father told Marc how hard it was getting through each day. The uncertainty, the worry, was tearing him apart. He would never forget the last time he saw his grandchildren, the previous February, when he'd come to Union for a visit. Alex was just six months old then, smiling and happy. Michael was running all over, getting into everything. He called him "Gran." Charles David Smith could still hear that little voice calling for Gran.

Marc Klaas left Union that night. He believed then that Susan Smith was clearly involved in the disappearance of her children. Nothing else made any sense. He had been in South Carolina for four days and had seen the couple just once, when they sped by him Saturday night in front of their Toney Road home trying to get away. There were no press conferences, no statements released to the media.

But Marc never believed Susan had harmed her children. *It's a custody battle,* he thought *as he caught his plane home. Everyone said she was a loving mother who doted on her children. They didn't seem to allow their personal differences to affect their parenting. It didn't seem they were using the children as weapons. She has those kids somewhere. And they're safe.*

David and Susan Smith arrive at the Union County Sheriff's office in Union, S.C., after Susan told police that a carjacker had taken her car and her children at gunpoint.
(ASSOCIATED PRESS/LOU KRASKY)

Susan Smith, in a 1988 high school yearbook photograph. (ASSOCIATED PRESS)

David Smith, who would be the father of Alex and Michael, in a 1988 high school yearbook photograph. (ASSOCIATED PRESS)

Tom Findlay (shown here in an undated photo) was Susan Smith's boyfriend until breaking up with her a week before Susan confessed to killing her two children. (ASSOCIATED PRESS)

Fourteen-month-old Alex and his three-year-old brother Michael smile as they celebrate Alex's first birthday in the summer of 1994. (ASSOCIATED PRESS/WNBC)

A sketch based upon Susan Smith's description of the person who stole her car and kidnapped her boys on October 25, 1994. (Associated Press/State Law Enforcement Division)

Diver Robert Stuckey searches John D. Long Lake near Union for clues to the missing Smith brothers. (Associated Press/Mary Ann Chastain)

Union County Sheriff Howard Wells *(right)* announces the arrest of Susan Smith. (ASSOCIATED PRESS/HEADLINE NEWS)

Barbara Benson, grandmother of the missing boys, turns from the television minutes after her son, David Smith, gave her the news of the boys' deaths.
(ASSOCIATED PRESS/MYRTLE BEACH SUN-NEWS, CECELIA KONYN)

Susan Smith covers her face as she leaves the York County Detention Center in Rock Hill, S.C., en route to her arraignment in Union. (ASSOCIATED PRESS/BOB JORDAN)

A white ribbon is thrown into John D. Long Lake in memory of the murdered Smith boys. (ASSOCIATED PRESS/LOU KRASKY)

A sign and flowers cover the coffin of the Smith brothers.
(ASSOCIATED PRESS/RUTH FREMSON)

David Smith breaks down at the funeral service for his sons.
(ASSOCIATED PRESS/ LOU KRASKY)

The casket is carried from the church.
(ASSOCIATED PRESS/MARY ANN CHASTAIN)

Beverly Russell and his wife Linda, mother of Susan Smith, leave the church following funeral services for their grandchildren. (ASSOCIATED PRESS/MARY ANN CHASTAIN)

11

On Monday night, six days after the disappearance of Michael and Alex Smith, Reverend Bob Cato called Mitchell Sinclair, the young man who Susan Smith had told police she was on her way to visit the night of the carjacking. Mitchell was a member of Cato's church, Fairview Baptist. In recent years, Cato had performed the funeral services for both of Mitchell's grandparents.

A few days earlier, Reverend Cato's son had told him surprising news.

"You know, Susan said she was going to Mitchell's house the night she was carjacked," he said.

"No," his father said slowly. "I did not know that."

The minister became concerned about Mitchell. He knew also that Mitchell was engaged to Donna Garner, Susan Smith's best friend. Perhaps the young couple needed help.

When he reached Mitchell, Cato explained the reason for his call.

"I can't image what you're going through," he said. "I'll be here for you. If you need to talk, give me a call."

Mitchell told Reverend Cato that the media were hounding him, loitering outside the house, and calling him at all hours of the day and night. When one reporter had finally cornered him, Mitchell had innocently remarked that "the truth will eventually come out." Now, he complained, the reporters seemed to think that he had something to do with the disappearance of the children. The sheriff had actually shot down the rumor that day, insisting at a press conference that Mitchell was not a suspect.

Mitchell couldn't really talk now, he explained to the pastor; he was on his way to work. He had third shift, 11:00 P.M. to 7:00 A.M. He thanked the minister for calling, and said he would be in touch shortly.

The next night, at 11:30 P.M., Reverend Cato heard a knock at the door. He'd already gone to bed, but he jumped up and hurried to the front hall.

It was Mitchell, his face pale under the porch light.

"Preacher, can we pray?" he asked.

"Sure," Cato said, kindly. "Come on in."

"All of us?" Mitchell asked.

Cato peered beyond Mitchell and saw a line of cars in the street, headlights shining.

"Yes. All of you."

One by one, sixteen members of the Smith and Russell families and several friends filed silently into Reverend Cato's living room. There was room for only ten on the couches and chairs; the rest settled on the carpet. Susan and David sat together on the floor, leaning back against the television.

For the next forty-five minutes, Rev. Cato spoke about God. He told the group about God's grace, and the special way God takes care of children. He talked about the soul and the body.

Susan told the minister that they would have a celebration when the babies came home. "I'll be there with bells on," he said, smiling.

At the end, one member of the group put it plainly: "We want the boys home."

The closest David Smith and the rest of his family came to believing the boys would come home was the following morning, when they learned that a child matching Alex's description had turned up in a Seattle motel room.

Sheriff Wells had gotten a call at 3:30 A.M. from officers in the Union police department. It was one of the first nights since the case began that he'd been home, catching a few hours sleep.

The officer told him about a call they'd received from Seattle police about a fourteen-month-old white child who matched a lot of the physical description of Alex Smith. "A lot of the clothing matches," the officer told him. "And the car is a South Carolina vehicle."

Wells hung up.

"What is it?" Wanda Wells asked.

"There's something happening and it's good, but that's all I can say," he said, his voice more upbeat then it had been for days. "I've got to get dressed and go."

Wanda didn't ask anything more. She knew her husband did not discuss details of his cases. In ten minutes, he'd taken a shower and shaved. She heard his car pull out of the driveway. Wanda lay in bed wondering about the lead. He'd called it promising. Wanda Wells hoped he was right.

The drive to his office took only five or ten minutes, but Sheriff Wells was more anxious than ever to get to his desk and begin making phone calls. *Maybe this is what we've been waiting for,* he thought as he pulled into the parking lot.

For the next few hours Wells tried to figure out exactly what was going on in Seattle. Law enforcement officials there were trying to do the same thing. Just before seven A.M., Wells decided to hold a brief press conference and announce his guarded optimism about a possible break in the case.

The reporters phoned their offices to ready the morning news shows for the report.

First, Wells called the Russell home. He didn't want the family to hear the news from the television. He told Bev Russell that they had something promising, but he couldn't tell them too much about it. He explained that he was about to give a brief press conference on the morning television news shows and that he would be in touch again as soon as he had more information.

Bev thanked the sheriff and quickly shared the news with the rest of the family. For a short time, David Smith thought that his prayers were about to be answered.

But the euphoria lasted only briefly. By ten A.M. word came from Seattle: the child was not Alex. The situation was suspicious: a man driving a car with South Carolina plates who claimed to be visiting his wife, who lived in Seattle, supposedly left their baby with a motel attendent, who then called police.

Sheriff Wells felt worse than he had at any point so far in the investigation. He had been so hopeful. For the first time, he had allowed himself to believe that the children of Susan Smith might be on their way home.

He picked up the phone and called Bev Russell. Wells's voice sounded so different than it had three hours before. He told Bev that he wanted the family to come in. "I need to give you the details about the early report we had," he said. "It's not going to work out for us, but I'll explain it." When Bev tried to ask questions, Wells cut him off. "I'll explain it all to you at one time."

When Howard Wells stepped outside into the sea of cameras and microphones, Wanda knew at once the news was bad. She had been working at her desk at Union Federal Savings Bank, half-listening to WBCU when she heard a press conference was scheduled for 10:00 A.M. As she had for the past eight days, she slipped out of her office and hurried to the kitchen, where the bank kept a television for its employees. *It's a wonder I don't get fired*, she thought as she waited impatiently for her husband to appear.

The bank was just across the street from the city hall where Wells's office was located, but Wanda prefered to watch her husband on the news. She didn't want to go over there, with all the crowds and reporters. She'd seen Howard more on television this week than she had in person.

When Howard Wells stepped up to the mircophone his wife saw right away by the expression on his face that the news was not good. She knew him well.

"Oh my goodness," she said softly to herself. "That wasn't the right child."

Wells spoke to the press, his voice strained. "New developments in the case are being checked as we speak. They are turning out not to be as promising as first anticipated. Our hopes have been high, but as the time goes by and we look into the case, there are a lot of similarities, there were a lot of things that really drew us close, our hearts soared for a while that we were close to recovering the children. That did not happen. We still have communications going on with the other agency, but I am of the belief that it is not going to affect our case. I was hoping it was the one we had been waiting on so long that was going to give us our direction and give us some breathing room that the children were okay and that we could get 'em back. The family was, like me, very excited. It's very hard when you get your hopes up to come back and see them dashed."

In his office, Wells spoke privately to the family: Bev and Linda, David and Susan, Margaret Gregory and her husband, and Scotty and Wendy. They crowded into his cramped office, gathering around his desk.

He told them how the information had come in and why they felt it had been promising. Then he told them how too many things were questionable. The bottom line was, the baby was not Alex.

When the family emerged from Wells's office, Margaret Frierson and Charlotte Foster were waiting outside. They'd gotten a call about the Seattle tip early that morning from the national office for the National Center for Missing and Exploited Children and had immediately driven to Union. But by the time they arrived, their hopes had been ended.

After their conversation with the sheriff, David and Susan stepped outside into a blur of cameras and lights. After ducking the press for a week, the young couple finally spoke.

Wearing windbreakers, hers white, his navy blue, they stepped forward awkwardly, their family and the sheriff surrounding them. Susan held her glasses and a photo of her sons in her left hand. David slipped his right arm around her waist, while his left hand held onto her left elbow.

Susan spoke first, her voice trembling with emotion.

"I would like to say that whoever has my children, that they please, that they please bring 'em home to us, where they belong. Our lives have been torn apart by the tragic events. I can't express how much they are wanted back home, how much we love 'em, we miss 'em. They are our hearts. I have prayed every day. There is not one minute that goes by that I don't think about those boys. And I have prayed that whoever has 'em, that the Lord will let them, let him, realize that they are missed and loved more than any children in this world, and that whoever has 'em, I pray every day that you're taking care of 'em, and know that we would do anything, anything to help you to get 'em home back to us. I just can't grasp it enough that we've just got to get 'em home. That's where they belong, with their Momma and Daddy."

David spoke next, his voice flatter, more monotone than his wife's had been.

"I would like to take the time to plead to the American public that you please do not give up on these two little boys, the search for their safe return home to us. That you continue to look for the car, our children, and for the suspects themselves, that you continue to keep your eyes open. And anything that you see that might help the police, call and let it be known. We ask that you continue to pray for me and my wife and for our family, but most of all that you continue to pray, that the American public continue to pray, for Michael and Alex, that they are returned home safely to their mother and father and the family members who love them so much, that you pray most of all for them and that they are being taken care of and that they are safe and that they will return home safely."

For a couple who had shied away from the media for almost a week, the two spoke freely.

When David had finished his appeal, Susan stepped up to the sea of microphones once more.

"I want to say to my babies that your Momma loves you so much, and your Daddy and this whole family loves you so much. And you guys have gotta be strong because I just know, I just feel in my heart that you're okay. You've got to take care of yourselves. And your Momma and Daddy are going to be right here waitin' on you when you get home. I love you so much."

She paused a moment, and then continued. "I want to tell a story. The night that this happened, before I left my house that night, Michael did something that he's never done before. He had his pooper [pacifier] in his mouth, and he came up to me and he took his pooper out, he put his arms around me and he told me, 'I love you so much, Momma.' He's always told me he loved me, but never, never before, not without me telling him first. And that was just . . . I'm holding on to that so much, because it means so much. I love 'em. I just can't express enough. I have been to the Lord in prayers every day with my family, by myself, with my husband. It just seems so unfair that somebody could take such two beautiful children. And I don't understand. I have put all my trust and faith in the Lord, that He's taking care of 'em, that He will bring them home to us."

Margaret Frierson and Charlotte Foster followed the family back to the Russell house. Inside, Margaret met David's mother, Barbara Benson, for the first time. Barbara had driven the four hours to Union from Garden City the weekend before.

Margaret tried to give the family a boost. "It's going to happen," she told them. "Yes, we're all disappointed but there will be another lead. Something else will come up."

She reminded them about the many cases she'd worked on where there was nothing, no calls, no leads, nothing. "At least people are calling in and care and are willing to make that call," she said. "There's nothing worse than those cases where nobody calls."

Back at the command center, SLED investigators and FBI agents watched Susan's emotional plea on television. Their scrutiny of the twenty-three-year-old secretary was intensifying. A day earlier, law-enforcement officials had searched her Toney Road home for the first time. Today, they would return.

As they listened to Susan make her emotional entreaty to the nameless, faceless man who had stolen her heart, her beautiful children, the investigators paid close attention to the words she chose, the catch in her voice. But, they noted, despite the emotion of the moment, she could not beckon the tears.

$$\left[\begin{array}{c} \textbf{12} \end{array}\right]$$

Now that Sheriff Wells and his team of investigators—SLED's chief, Robert Stewart, SLED behavioral specialist David Caldwell, Pete Logan, a retired FBI agent, now an investigator for SLED, and Jim Oppy, Special Agent in Charge of South Carolina, had concluded that Susan Smith was lying about her children they faced a daunting task: proving it and uncovering the truth.

They continued to interview Susan daily and gradually began to suggest to her that while they wanted to believe her story, they couldn't. Early on in the interrogations, one of the investigators flatly accused Susan of doing in her children.

Her reaction stunned the men. The docile, weeping girl who kept praying for "God to look after my babies," suddenly turned angry, shouting at her accuser. Susan's peppery comeback taught them two things: that Susan Smith was not just a sweet brokenhearted mother but also a strong-willed young woman—and that this hardened suspect would be tough to crack.

Her story about the carjacking had plenty of holes. The red light, the absence of cars at the intersection, her conflicting stories about where she was going that night and where she had been. And ultimately, that the burgundy Mazda never turned up.

"The problem was," said one senior investigator, "it was nothing that could be proven. It just didn't ring right. We knew she was lying about it."

Because the investigators could not prudently ignore Susan's possible culpability from the start, and because they felt that she had probably acted alone, the team had to consider that the car, and maybe the children, were somewhere within walking distance of the McCloud house.

"We kept going back, kept going back to within two miles of the McCloud place," says an investigator. "We couldn't understand why we didn't find that car."

From the start, the men carried out a meticulously planned interrogation campaign to gradually break down Susan Smith's defenses and encourage her to confess. Every day's movements were carefully scripted. There were no ad libbed entrances; no casual questions to Susan that had not been planned beforehand.

To some extent, Pete Logan and Sheriff Wells served as the "good" cops. Logan, a graying, grandfatherly type, spoke gently to Susan, yet shrewdly managed to manipulate her into trusting him at the same time.

The interrogators hoped to build on Susan's trust in them to coax her into confessing. And they were careful never to push her too hard. If they did, they feared, she might become defensive and clam up, or worse yet, commit suicide. They knew of her past attempts at killing herself and they knew if she died, they might never find the children.

All still fervently hoped the boys would be found alive, but in their hearts, they knew that wish seemed less and less likely to come true.

The strongest tool against Susan's steadfast claim that she, indeed, was a victim of a carjacker was psychology. Investigators met several times a day, often with technical experts like Caldwell, to consider the next move.

"The timing was everything: what we were going to do, when we were going to do it, who would be responsible," an investigator said.

Investigators met with Susan at two different locations—so-called safe houses—away from the prying eyes of the media. Reporters kept trying to read their actions. It wouldn't help if they began asking why investigators continued to question Susan. They moved the command post into a Union recreation center at one point, and then to another location later.

After the first confrontation with Susan right after she told the carjacking story failed to break her, Logan, fifty-nine, met daily with Susan, talking gently to her and asking her to go over and over the events of October 25. After each conversation, he would hook her up to the polygraph and test her. She routinely failed the most critical question: "Do you know where your children are?"

On more than one occasion, investigators felt sure Susan was about to break. She would stop her conversation, lay her head on her arms on the table and sit, silent and still.

"She showed a lot of characteristic traits of one who was about to break," one of the investigators said.

But then, Susan would abruptly sit upright, and steadfastly repeat her story.

The behavioral specialists who analyzed Susan Smith began to put together a profile of a cool, cunning woman with a strong drive to succeed. Early on in the investigation, Tom Findlay had provided the investigators with a copy of the letter he had sent Susan, ending their relationship. He told them Susan had reacted vindictively to his rebuff, with a bitterness that surprised him. With this information, and their own firsthand knowledge of her angry outburst when confronted with their early suspicions, investigators began to put together a possible motive: that greed and ambition had pushed her to rid herself of her children.

It was SLED's David Caldwell who designed a series of ploys for Pete Logan to use in the lengthy conversations he had with Susan Smith almost daily. Several of the ploys would be used over the course of the week-long interrogation as part of their efforts to pressure Susan into confessing.

One of the teams' first ideas was to develop a no-holds-barred media blitz.

Of course, already Union was teeming with reporters. Satellite trucks choked Main Street and friends and family of Susan and David Smith were being inundated with requests for interviews. The tabloids, both print and television, offered money for information, and the story, it seemed, couldn't get any more attention.

But while reporters from all over the country chased the story some of the coverage was being carefully crafted by the team of investigators.

On Tuesday night, November 1, exactly one week after Susan made her claims about the carjacker, Wells met with dozens of reporters in the parking lot of the courthouse. His timing seemed symbolic. His words were carefully chosen, impeccably planned. And no mistake about it, they were directed to one specific listener: Susan Smith.

"I don't know that we're any closer to finding the car," he began. "I have nothing encouraging. We're following old information that we've just not gotten to. I don't think it's developed into anything as of yet to be any more excited about than yesterday."

He talked about the abductor—the man whose phone call he said he awaited. "I'm waiting right now, hopefully to hear from the abductors," Wells told the group. "I will talk with him directly. I will go to where he is or I will go to where I can find the children. I'm open to suggestions right now, and I'm hoping he will call. This case has grown to such a degree that if this abductor has seen the amount of attention that has been placed on it, that he would be frightful of how to handle himself or what to do or even to move right now.

"We're still taking it as we did at the beginning, as a random carjacking. We do not know why the subject was interested in this particular car or if it had any bearing whatsoever, why the abductor would be at this particular location or even if he was one of our own citizens or not. We are following different scenarios: if it was a single abductor, what would be necessary to keep us from finding the vehicle, and where he might be.

"We've looked at scenarios that would involve

two abductors and we've looked at scenarios that would involve more than two abductors, trying to figure what their plan of action might have been, how far they were willing to go to secrete this vehicle or where they may be at this time."

Sheriff Wells looked intently into the cameras. "It's very easy to believe Susan Smith, that one person took her at gun point but it's also reasonable to believe that maybe someone else also was involved, who was picked up later or someone else was waiting to be picked up or someone else assisted in hiding the car. When I say, 'two or more people' it does not mean anything different than what she said, that one took the car.

"I wish I could tell you right now that I had something that made me very confident and had taken some of the burden off of our hearts, but as of right now, I don't have anything that gives me a great deal of relief. I can't say that anything is very promising at this time."

In the investigators' plan to intensify the media spotlight and unnerve Susan Smith, one unwitting participant was none other than Shirley McCloud.

On the Tuesday that Sheriff Wells faced the press, Roger Gregory, the captain of the sheriff's department, called Shirley McCloud. He told her that the sheriff had asked if she would be willing to be interviewed for a segment to be shown that weekend on the syndicated television show *America's Most Wanted.* The program would highlight the carjacking case, and hopefully, bring in the tip they needed to find Susan Smith's children.

Shirley was not pleased about the idea of telling her story on television, but she tried to hide her lack of enthusiasm. She told the captain she would do it.

The *America's Most Wanted* people came that night, setting up a makeshift studio in the McCloud's den. Shirley had asked the captain to be there for the taping, and he was. In fact, he, too, was interviewed on the show. Like Shirley, the captain said that he did not believe Susan Smith had done anything to her children.

If the investigators were so sure by then that Susan was lying to them, why tape a show insisting on her innocence?

It is likely that they were hoping that the more media attention given to the story of the missing children, the more pressure would be brought to bear on Susan and the more likely she would break down.

Their next step was appealing to the carjacker publicly. The investigators arranged for calls to go out to a handful of the city's most influential ministers. They were all asked to gather on the steps of the courthouse on Thursday evening to make an emotional plea to the man who stole Susan Smith's babies.

Rev. Long was invited, as was Rev. Cato. The Reverend A. J. Brackett came to represent St. Paul Baptist Church. In all, almost twenty clergyman were asked to meet at the steps of the courthouse. They all said they would be there.

During the second week of the search, SLED's David Caldwell came up with the most elaborate ploy of all:

Investigators reportedly would use desktop publishing to print up what would appear to be an authentic newspaper story about a young mother who had killed her children, then served a short sentence, and had, on release, made a fine new life for herself by marrying a wealthy physician. A photograph of a policewoman Susan didn't know would be used as an illustration of the woman. It was aimed at convincing Susan to confess and take her medicine in expectation of a good life to follow.

They never used the ruse. The *America's Most Wanted* piece never aired. And the Union ministers who gathered that day in front of all the cameras at the courthouse but did not have an opportunity to appeal to the carjacker.

Because just after three P.M. on Thursday, November 3, Susan Vaughan Smith confessed to the murder of her two children.

13

On the day Susan Smith admitted to rolling her car into John D. Long Lake, her two boys trapped in their car seats, she began the morning by proclaiming defiantly on all three network morning shows that she had had nothing to do with the disappearance of her children.

She and David were up by five that day, getting ready for the invasion of television cameras into the living room of the Russell home. They sat together on the couch, holding hands.

Susan did most of the talking.

"I don't think any parent could love my children more than I do, and I would never even think about doing anything that would harm them," she said. "The truth has been told. I know what the truth is and I did not have anything to do with the abduction of my children.

"It's painful to have the finger pointed at you when it's your children. Whoever did this is a sick and emotionally unstable person. I can't imagine why anyone would want to take our children."

On *CBS This Morning*, anchor Harry Smith asked David if he believed Susan.

"I believe my wife totally," David said softly.

Added Susan, "It hurts to know that I may be accused. I do not understand why they would do what they are doing. Our lives have been torn apart by this tragic event. I can't express how much they are wanted back home."

Shortly after the broadcast, a family member called the *Union Daily Times*, canceling an exclusive interview and photo shoot they'd promised reporter Anna Brown and photographer Tim Kimzey. Susan and David had had enough media pressure for the day. The couple, exhausted, retired to a back bedroom for a nap.

Susan's friend from Conso, Toni Horne, dropped by briefly on her lunch hour. "They've just got to find my babies," Susan told her. "They've got to bring my babies back."

Around 12:30 P.M., Susan Smith left the Russell home. She told David she was going to drop off some letters. She did not tell him that Sheriff Wells had sent for her to take her to another safe house for yet another round of questioning by interrogators.

In the dining room of the Russell house, Margaret Frierson and Charlotte Foster were manning phones and discussing the possibility of arranging for Charles David Smith, David's father, to speak on NBC's *Dateline* show. They were also sorting through the dozens of requests the family and the Adam Walsh Center had received from strangers offering to put up reward money for the safe return of Michael and Alex Smith. Margaret had asked Sheriff Wells about setting up a reward, but he had asked her to wait.

"Not right now," he told her. "At this point in the investigation, we don't want to do it."

For a few days, Margaret put off answering the requests, but by Thursday she felt she could no longer wait. Out of respect for the donors, she needed to respond to their generous offers.

Margaret planned to write an individual letter to each person who called or wrote in, explaining that they did not plan to set up a reward fund now, but might in the future. She would ask the donors to let them know in writing how much money they would be able to give.

A little past three P.M., Margaret and Charlotte explained the situation to David, Bev, and Linda. They told the family they would be working out of their Columbia office for the rest of the day.

The family said they understood, and thanked them for coming.

Just before they left, Margaret and Charlotte

said good-bye to Doug and Susan Smith, David's uncle and aunt. Doug Smith is Charles David Smith's brother. They had all been staying at Susan and David's Toney Road house since the children disappeared.

But with so little progress in the search for Michael and Alex Doug and Susan were preparing to return home to Michigan. They promised to fly back to South Carolina at a moment's notice if there were any developments in the case.

The Russell house was filled, as usual. Susan's brother Scotty Vaughan was there, but his wife, Wendy, was not. After a week's leave of absence, she had finally gone back to work. Several women from Buffalo United Methodist Church had arrived in the afternoon, carrying trays of hot food for the family. Some of the local ministers were on their way to the Russells'. They planned to give the family a brief summary of their upcoming appeal to the carjacker.

By now, the family had seen that afternoon's edition of the *Union Daily Times.* In an interview, Shirley McCloud had spoken out in defense of Susan, insisting that Susan's panic the night of October 25 was genuine, and that she was thoroughly convinced that Susan Smith was telling the truth.

Shirley had tried to duck the interview but reporter Anna Brown had persisted. "Shirley, everybody's been saying Susan said this or that, but you know what she said that night," Anna had told her. "You could set the story straight for the people of Union."

Shirley had given in. She had decided Anna was probably right. But she had made one request: she wanted to see the article before it ran. Anna agreed, faxing her an early version. Shirley read it over carefully, making a few minor changes. When she was satisfied she gave Anna the go-ahead.

Once again, Shirley McCloud faced the public and defended the young woman whose trembling face she'd held tenderly in her hands on that horrible night. It was, Shirley McCloud had ultimately decided, her responsibility to fight for Susan. As the days passed and no word of the little boys emerged, Shirley could not forget how frail and lost Susan had seemed that night, her body trembling as she sat hunched over on Shirley's couch, sobbing with her head ducked practically between her knees. Others didn't know, Shirley reasoned. They weren't in the living room at nine o'clock that Tuesday. They didn't see what Shirley saw.

And so the stalwart face of a trusting Shirley McCloud made the front page of the local newspaper the very day that Susan Smith broke down and said that everything had been a lie.

Investigators will not reveal what they said to Susan Smith on the afternoon of November 3,

1994, but it appears that their unremitting pressure, the media bombardment, and perhaps a touch of her own conscience had at last pushed Susan Smith over the edge. They also reportedly confronted her with all the inconsistencies in her story and told her they planned to go public with their suspicions. Then, Wells went in to talk privately to Susan. After so many hours of meetings and strategy sessions, even the investigators found themselves a bit surprised when Susan Smith at last admitted the terrible fate she had brought on her two young sons.

Susan had seemed much the same as she showed up for questioning that day. Dressed in jeans and a hooded sweatshirt, she hadn't appeared particularly agitated when the sheriff arranged for her to be picked up at the Russell home that afternoon. But something within her had clearly changed.

Within two hours Susan Smith began to tell Sheriff Howard Wells what happened on the night of October 25.

Susan Smith talked about the crushing isolation she felt as she drove her Mazda along the dark highway, consumed by the desire to end her life. She had left home that evening planning to drive around for a while and then take the boys to her mother's house.

But the bad feelings inside her soul ached so much. No one, she felt, could help her, and nothing could be worse than how she felt at that very moment. Susan talked about how wrong her whole life seemed, and how she could not escape the torment she felt inside. She tallied the ills in her life, recalling events as far back as the abortion she'd had while she was in high school.

Susan told the investigators about Tom Findlay, how much she loved him, how badly it hurt that he didn't love her back. She admitted to them that she had done something to him after he'd ended their relationship—something she believed was so awful she was convinced that he could never love her.

In her confession, Susan Smith maintained that she pulled off Highway 49 onto the dark, windy road that led to John D. Long Lake because she was ready to die. As for her children, Susan said that she believed they would be better off with her, with God, than left motherless and alone.

In her plan, it would be the three of them—Susan, Michael, and Alex. They would die together.

Susan told the investigators that she tried to end their lives that night. She put the car in neutral and let it roll down the boat ramp but then she stopped. She tried again, and again, she stopped.

She told them she got out of the car, overcome with grief, racked with pain. All the time, the babies slept so peacefully in the back seat, not a sound from either one of them.

Susan Smith avowed that she had reached the lowest point in her life. It was then that she reached into the car and released the emergency brake.

During her confession, Susan repeatedly told the authorities that she loved her sons, that she never meant for this to happen, and that she was so very, very sorry. After it had happened, she told them, she wanted so badly to take back what she'd done but she knew that wasn't possible. And so she ran, screaming hysterically. When she wound up on the front porch of Shirley and Rick McCloud's house, her alibi was already in the works.

Keeping the terrible secret these nine days had been torture, she insisted. Watching the pain her parents were suffering, the agony endured by David and his parents, cut her deeply. She said she was scared but admitted that she always knew that her story would eventually collapse, that the truth of what she did that night at the lake would inevitably emerge.

Now that it had, Susan Smith felt enormously relieved.

For Sheriff Howard Wells, Susan Smith's confession confirmed what in his heart he'd already known—that she had indeed killed those precious boys. Yet as he listened to her talk, the brutality of her actions rendered him almost unable to speak.

For a moment, he was paralyzed by his horror of what Susan had done. But only for a moment. There was so much to do, not a moment to waste.

After nine days of nothing but theories, speculations, and questions, Sheriff Howard Wells had finally gotten some answers. Now, the next step was to confirm them.

Outside Susan's earshot, Wells met with SLED Chief Robert Stewart and FBI Agent Jim Oppy. The men, their faces drawn with sadness after learning of the grim news, hunkered down to strategize their next, pivotal steps. They contrived a plan for confirming Susan's story and then breaking the news to the family. They called the divers they would need to scour the bottom of John D. Long lake, the patrol units they would need to block off the road to the lake while they conducted their search. The family, they knew, would need to be told of Susan's confession in person, but they didn't want to deliver the sad news until they had made sure that the Mazda and the two Smith boys were indeed resting in those murky waters. And they knew the always-difficult task of informing a family about the death of a loved one would be complicated by the glare of the media. Reporters and camera crews would swarm to the crime scene as soon as word got out. The citizens of Union, anxious to know what was going on, would likely not be far behind.

Once their plan was in motion, Union County Sheriff Howard Wells left Susan in the custody of SLED agents and stepped outside into the sunshine. He got into his car and drove directly to the lake, traveling along Highway 49. It was, in essence, the same drive he'd made nine days before, when he responded to Rick McCloud Jr.'s frantic call.

He didn't think about that now, about the irony of the words emitted from the radio that night.

Wells did not know what would happen over the next few hours. It had been nine long days since the lawman had taken on the toughest case of his career, a case that had catapulted him into a national spotlight. Now the end of the investigation was approaching, the worst finish he could have imagined.

Soon he would have almost all the answers to the questions that dogged him for so long. Except, of course, the most commanding one: Why?

He wondered if even Susan knew.

By the time Wells left the safe house, Susan had been handed a pen and a notebook and been asked to put her confession in writing.

She filled two pages with her carefully crafted script, rounding off her letters with neat flourishes and drawing in little hearts whenever she wanted to use the word "heart":

When I left my home on Tuesday, October 25, I was very emotionally distraught. I didn't want to live anymore! I felt like things could never get any worse. When I left home, I was going to ride around a little while and then go to my mom's.

As I rode and rode and rode, I felt even more anxiety coming upon me about not wanting to live. I felt I couldn't be a good mom anymore, but I didn't want my children to grow up without a mom. I felt I had to end our lives to protect us from any grief or harm.

I had never felt so lonely and so sad in my entire life. I was in love with someone very much, but he didn't love me and never would. I had a very difficult time accepting that. But I had hurt him very much and I could see why he could never love me.

When I was at John D. Long Lake, I had never felt so scared and unsure as I did then. I wanted to end my life so bad and was in my car ready to go down that ramp into the water, and I did go part way, but I stopped. I went again and stopped. I then got out of the car and stood by the car a nervous wreck.

Why was I feeling this? Why was everything so bad in my life? I had no answers to these questions. I dropped to the lowest point when I allowed my children to go down that ramp into the water without me.

I took off running and screaming, "Oh God! Oh God, NO! What have I done? Why did you let this happen? I wanted to turn around so bad and go back, but I knew it was too late. I was an absolute mental case! I couldn't believe what I had done.

I love my children with all my heart and that will never change. I have prayed to them for forgiveness and hope that they will find it in their heart to forgive me. I never meant to hurt them!! I am sorry for what has happened and I know that I need some help. I don't think I will ever be able to forgive myself for what I have done.

My children, Michael and Alex, are with our Heavenly Father now, and I know that they will never be hurt again. As a mom, that means more than words can ever say.

I knew from day one, the truth would prevail, but I was so scared I didn't know what to do. It was very tough emotionally to sit and watch my family hurt like they did. It was time to bring a peace of mind to everyone, including myself.

My children deserve to have the best, and now they will. I broke down on Thursday November 3, and told Sheriff Howard Wells the truth. It wasn't easy, but after the truth was out, I felt like the world was lifted off my shoulders.

I know now that it is going to be a tough and long road ahead of me. At this very moment, I don't feel I will be able to handle what's coming, but I have prayed to God that he give me the strength to survive each day and to face those times and situations in my life that will be extremely painful. I have put my total faith in God, and He will take care of me.

Susan V. Smith
11/3/94
5:05 P.M.

14

Despite Howard Wells's carefully scripted plans, word of Susan's confession leaked almost immediately.

A few minutes past four P.M. on November 3, the Associated Press began reporting that Susan Smith had confessed to the murder of her sons, and that law-enforcement troops were heading to John D. Long Lake. Television stations nationwide broke into regularly scheduled programming to announce the latest developments. At WBCU in Union, news director William Christopher began advising county residents of the AP report, but he stressed repeatedly that the information was unconfirmed.

Phone calls from both the media and individual citizens flooded into the Union County Sheriff's Office. Wells sent word to his staff to announce a press conference, scheduled for 5:00 P.M.

Even before then, a large crowd had been gathering for the previously scheduled appeal by the county's ministers for the carjacker to release the Smith boys. More than 100 locals and journalists were already on hand.

In a short time, hundreds more would gather in the street as they learned the horrible fate of the children they had come to love.

Once Wells and his team set their plan in motion, scores of law-enforcement officials around the state began to get the word.

Just after three P.M., one of the first calls came into the sheriff's command post that had been set up in a Union recreation center several days after the alleged carjacking. It was almost always saturated with SLED agents and deputy sheriffs, picking up new assignments, reporting in to their superiors, or just taking breaks, catching up on the latest developments in the case.

This time, the assignment was ominous. Mike Gault, a corporal with the South Carolina Department of Natural Resources, and SLED agent Spike McGraw got their orders: secure John D. Long Lake.

The two men did not ask questions. They took one of the wildlife department's four-wheel drive trucks and headed north on Highway 49. On their way to the lake, they stopped at a friend's house. The man had offered the use of his johnboat, a small aluminum craft, if law enforcement needed it. Gault and McCraw picked it up and loaded it in the back of the truck.

Meanwhile, wildlife dispatchers were rounding up four of the department's nine divers, all of whom had searched for the Mazda in Union rivers, ponds, and lakes over the previous week.

As he headed to the lake, Mike Gault picked up his radio and called Steve Morrow, a conservation officer with the South Carolina Natural Resources Department and one of the state's divers, whom he knew well. Morrow, he learned, had already received his orders to meet law enforcement at John D. Long Lake. Morrow told Gault he was on his way from Spartanburg.

"How long will it be until you get there?" Gault asked.

Morrow estimated he could be at the lake in about twenty minutes.

"You probably should hurry up," Gault said.

Morrow said he would.

As Steve Morrow picked up speed toward Highway 49, the thirty-eight-year-old sergeant began to think that this was more than a routine search. When the dispatcher had given him his orders a short time earlier, he hadn't realized that this might be the day they finally found some answers.

It was actually Morrow's day off. That morning, he'd been at his home in Gaffney, about thirty miles northwest of Union, when his office phoned, telling him he needed to attend a preliminary hearing in Spartanburg. The hearing was on a case of a man Morrow had recently arrested for deer hunting at night. Morrow had changed clothes quickly and rushed to his pickup. When he got in, he had realized the truck was low on gas. He'd grabbed the keys to his dive van instead.

Morrow made it to the hearing in time to testify and was on his way home when the call came in from the dispatcher. At this point, he was thankful he'd taken the van. Now, he didn't need to waste time stopping at home to pick up his wet suit and other dive equipment.

Morrow pressed the accelerator of the van and drove a bit faster. Last night, he'd watched Susan and David Smith on television, pleading for the return of their children. He'd seen the photo again of Michael and Alex. Little Michael, he kept thinking, was just a year younger than his own boy.

As he sped down the highway that day, Steve Morrow wondered what awaited him in the waters of John D. Long Lake.

When diver Curtis Jackson got his call to report to the lake he was en route to Blacksburg from his home in Gaffney. The wildlife department had had reports of deer hunters using bait to lure the animals into a favorable position, violating South Carolina law. Jackson's assignment was to stop them.

But when the call came in, the dispatcher didn't mince words.

"Get to Union," he said. "Don't talk to nobody, don't use your cellular phone. Just go. They've got something."

Jackson quickly returned to his home to pick up some rope then headed for John D. Long Lake. He was among the first divers to arrive there. Even the sheriff had not yet appeared.

Mike Gault filled Jackson in on the details. By the time he was done, Sheriff Howard Wells and his team of investigators were on the scene.

Wells told Jackson that reporters would likely be arriving soon and it was going to be difficult to keep them out. He needed Jackson to accomplish three things: locate the car, determine whether the bodies of the children were, indeed, inside, and lastly, mark the site with an anchor.

He revealed to the young diver what Susan had told him about the car. It rolled in; it had not been driven in fast, as they had originally assumed when they first considered the possibility that the Mazda was at the bottom of the lake.

Curtis Jackson felt the pressure of his grave assignment. He was one of the newer members of the wildlife team; he'd joined the department four years earlier. Since then he'd dived for cars, bodies, and weapons, but never in a case as

high profile and emotionally charged as this
one.

Sheriff Wells stepped back while Jackson and
Mike Gault stood on the banks of the lake and
used a compass to note the direction in which
the boat ramp leads to the water. Once the men
were submerged in the dark waters they would
need to organize their search toward that heading. The men pushed the johnboat into the
water and began to paddle. As they made their
way out, Steve Morrow pulled up in his van. He
took one look at Howard Wells and knew that
they weren't only looking for a car, they were
searching for the missing children.

Morrow had known Wells for years. Back
when Wells was a conservation officer, the two
had worked on many cases together. Like Wells,
Morrow was a Union native. He'd even graduated in the same high school class as Wanda
Wells.

Standing beside his old friend, Steve Morrow
watched as Curtis Jackson lowered himself out
of the johnboat and into the cold, murky water
of John D. Long Lake. Like the other solemn-
faced lawmen lining the shore, he stood grim
and silent as they waited for events to unfold.

They knew it might take a while. Divers traditionally do not come up unless they have either
found what they were looking for, or are running out of air. Jackson had enough oxygen
for at least an hour. Sheriff Wells had advised

Jackson to look toward the right of what they believed would be the car's likely trajectory off the boat ramp. But after fruitlessly searching that area, Jackson surfaced and swam over to the johnboat.

From the shore, the men could see Gault and Jackson talking. Gault, in the boat, told the diver some more of the details of what Susan Smith had told the sheriff. Armed with new information, Jackson went back down. This time it took him just six minutes to find the car.

He could make out some colors but little else. His hand touched the car's underside. He was not surprised to find that the car had overturned. He knew that as an object sinks, the heaviest part goes first. In the case of the Mazda, the weight of the engine caused it to flip over, its roof settling at the bottom.

But his assignment was not complete. Jackson swam to the window and tried to peer inside. He raised his dive light, pressing it against the glass, but still, he saw only blackness. He cursed the weak battery in his light; he could see only about eight inches in front of him.

Curtis Jackson surfaced again at five P.M. When Sheriff Wells and the others saw him emerge from the water, they knew he'd found something. He waited impatiently as Mike Gault dropped a marker to Jackson, who went down again and attached it to the car. On the surface, a plastic milk jug floated about 100 feet out into

John D. Long Lake, a bleak marker of the final resting place of Michael and Alex Smith. Everyone had been in such a hurry to get the search underway, they hadn't had time to locate a traditional anchor. The makeshift one, Jackson figured, would have to do. He'd rigged it up as he drove to the lake that day.

Jackson swam to the shore. Wells met him at the water's edge.

"Did you see them in there?" he asked.

Jackson shook his head. "The light wasn't bright enough," he explained. "The battery is fixing to go and it wasn't going to go through glass."

Wells nodded. He understood, but he still needed his answer.

Jackson didn't go back down. By now, Steve Morrow and Francis Mitchum from Somerville were on hand. Both Morrow and Mitchum were sergeants and Jackson was only a corporal. He would be left behind.

The new divers didn't bother with the johnboat. They waded into the water and swam to the marker. With their more sophisticated dive lights, the men were able to see inside the Mazda.

When they came up, they were crying.

When Sheriff Wells got the confirmation he needed he moved quickly from the lakeshore to the waiting SLED helicopter. It lifted off and headed directly south, landing less than five minutes later on the front lawn of a young couple who lived two doors away from the Russells on Heathwood Road.

By the time Howard Wells entered the Russell home the family had already heard the AP report that Susan had confessed to killing the children. They were braced for the worst. When Sheriff Russell walked through the front door of the Russell home, his expression told them all they needed to know. David Smith, who at twenty-four had lost his precious children, began to scream and run wildly around the room in total anguish.

Sheriff Wells stayed about twenty minutes at the Russell home. As he always did, the lawman kept his emotions in check. Somehow, he had to get through the next few hours.

He told the sobbing family members parts of what Susan had said in her confession, and how they had confirmed her account of driving the Mazda, with the two little boys strapped inside, into John D. Long lake. He informed them that she had been arrested and charged with two counts of murder. A bail hearing would be arranged for the following day at the Union County Courthouse.

Before he left, Sheriff Wells told the family that he had arranged a press conference. In a few minutes, he would announce to the world the deaths of Michael and Alex Smith, and the arrest of their mother.

Wells sprinted back to the helicopter. By now, several of the Russells' neighbors had gathered on their front lawn, their faces drawn with dread. They heard the whirling sounds of the SLED helicopter, seen the devastating report on television. Now, they looked at Sheriff Howard Wells and they knew it was true.

The sheriff put out his hand and one of the neighbors clasped it, giving it a squeeze.

"I'm sorry for landing in your yard," Howard Wells said quietly.

He got into the helicopter. A minute later, he was gone.

Margaret Frierson and Charlotte Foster were on Interstate 26, just outside of Columbia, when their mobile phone rang. Both women were startled. The phone worked only sporadically—in Union it never seemed to work at all—and besides they almost never received calls on the mobile, they just made them.

On the line was Julie Cartwright, Coordinator of Public Affairs for the National Center for Missing and Exploited Children in Washington, D.C. Cartwright had just received a call from a reporter with a stunning question.

"Margaret, we've gotten information that Susan Smith has confessed and her children are dead," Cartwright said bluntly. "Can you confirm or deny?"

Margaret swallowed hard. She and Charlotte had been chatting nonstop in the car ever since they left the Russells' home less than an hour earlier. They hadn't bothered to turn on the radio. Margaret could hardly believe what she was hearing.

"At this point, I can't do either," she told Cartwright, slowly. "I will do that as soon as I can."

She explained that she was on the interstate in her car, but that they would stop as soon as possible and get to a phone to call SLED. She didn't want to use the mobile phone for a call like this.

The women thought about stopping at a friend's home who lived nearby, but decided to simply head in to the Adam Walsh Center offices. They needed privacy to try to verify the latest developments.

Within a few minutes, they had pulled into a parking space and unlocked the door of their modest first-floor office in downtown Columbia. Charlotte snapped on the television as Margaret dialed the number for the SLED office. When she finally reached an official there, he was reluctant to confirm the report. The sheriff would be making his announcement very soon, he told her.

Margaret didn't push. She thanked the agent and hung up.

Like everyone else, they waited.

When Shirley McCloud and a friend returned home from work on the evening of November 3, Highway 49 was blocked off, with yellow police tape strung along the sides for several hundred yards. A deputy sheriff stood in the McCloud's driveway, motioning to cars to continue passing. Shirley's friend, who had given her a ride to and from work that day, pulled in beside the deputy.

"Who are you?" the cop asked brusquely.

"I live here," Shirley said.

"Well, go on in."

"What's going on?"

The cop did not answer.

Rick McCloud and his son had both arrived home an hour earlier, at about 4:30. Since then, father and son had joined dozens of onlookers at the bottom of the road, across from the entrance to John D. Long Lake.

Shirley stepped out of her friend's van and looked up, startled. Her aunt was standing on the front porch. The older woman had been driving home from work when she heard the AP report of Susan's confession on the radio. She had noticed that her niece's car wasn't in the driveway, and decided to wait for her.

As Shirley walked up the path, her aunt gave her the news.

"Shirley, they say that Susan has confessed," she said.

Shirley McCloud stopped cold. She followed her aunt into the house, and abruptly slammed the front door.

"Confessed to what?" she barked. "She hasn't done anything."

Shirley's aunt touched her sleeve and moved her aside.

"Shirley, open the door so I can tell Kathy," she said.

Shirley's friend Kathy stood awkwardly on the porch. Shirley's aunt invited her in.

Inside, Shirley McCloud was livid.

"She hasn't done anything," she repeated. "This is just a rumor. They're just back down there doing that lake again to find nothing."

"Shirley," her aunt continued, "I am just telling you what the TV is saying. The Associated Press says that Susan Smith has confessed to killing her children."

"I don't care," her niece shot back. "Until I hear Sheriff Wells say that she has confessed I do not believe it. This woman did not kill her children."

"Okay," her aunt said. "We'll wait."

The TV was already on. It showed the scene at the courthouse, with the crowd waiting for Sheriff Wells.

Shirley's husband came in, slightly out of breath. Once he'd seen Kathy's van pull up he'd sprinted back to the house. Rick Jr. remained at the roadside.

"Rick, she didn't do it," Shirley said immediately.

"No," Rick said, slowly. "I can't believe it either."

But Rick McCloud's eyes said something else. He now suspected that they had been wrong, very wrong about Susan Vaughan Smith.

"Rick," Shirley repeated, "she did not do it. She did not."

This time, Rick just shook his head. If the news was bad, he knew his wife was going to take it very, very hard.

Eight miles away, the SLED helicopter had made the short trip from the Russells' and was landing at a ballfield around the corner from the sheriff's office. SLED had been using the field as a helicopter pad for the past nine days.

When Howard Wells walked into the parking lot of city hall at 6:45 P.M. the blaze of lights and cameras was nearly blinding. Hundreds of townspeople waited anxiously to hear what he had to say. The ministers, too, were all on hand. They had gotten word not long before that there was no longer any need for them to appeal to the carjacker.

While the scene from the city hall played on

all the major networks, across the street at the bank, Wanda Wells caught her breath. She and six of her co-workers had heard about the press conference on WBCU and had been waiting since five P.M. They could hear the commotion just outside the door on Main Street as satellite trucks passed by and people called out to each other in the street.

As Sheriff Wells prepared to speak to millions of Americans that night, Wanda Wells took one look at the man she married seventeen years earlier and knew that he would say: the worst had occurred.

15

"I have a brief statement to make," Sheriff Howard Wells said. "When I am finished, there will be no questions asked, and none answered."

In the glare of the lights in the city hall parking lot, Sheriff Wells paused for just a moment. His declaration would soon stun the nation, but here in Union, he knew, his words would unleash a cascade of emotions. In the early evening hours of November 3, this forty-one-year-old lawman would have to break the heart of his own hometown.

And he could give them neither comfort, nor even an explanation. He came armed only with facts, ones that he had proven, the evidence that he believed in. He could only tell them what he knew, what was real.

"Susan Smith," Sheriff Wells said loudly, his voice cracking and echoing in the night air, "has been arrested and charged with two counts of murder in connection with the deaths of her children, Michael, three, and Alexander, fourteen months."

A gasp went up in the crowd.

Wells continued. "Late this afternoon, a car was located in John D. Long Lake. Two bodies were found in the vehicle's back seat. Mrs. Smith has been arrested and will be charged with two counts of murder. Identities are still pending."

With that, Sheriff Howard Wells turned and left the sea of people outside the Union County Courthouse reeling from the news he had just delivered. Chief Stewart was at his heels. The lawman had told the world that the search for Michael and Alex Smith was over. Now, he steeled himself for the most brutal task of all: raising the car from the dark waters.

The tears in Union that night fell in living rooms, and groceries stores, in the churches were people stopped to pray, and in cars where drivers listened to the simple, succinct words that said that the unthinkable had occurred, and that it had taken place right here in Union.

The tears fell in the crowds who'd gathered on Main Street that night, some caught unabashedly in the glare of camera lights and broadcast to the nation, the pain of a small town reaching out to a grieving nation. They fell in the living room of Dot and Earl Frost, in the den of Shirley and Rick McCloud, in the bank kitchen where Wanda Wells and her friends embraced, unable to speak or even to close up and go home, and in the bedroom at the home of Carlisle and Georgia Henderson, who that night knelt down to pray to the God they believed would keep those little souls safe, at last.

Rick McCloud was once again standing at the edge of his driveway along the closed-off section of Highway 49 when Sheriff Wells made his stunning announcement. After listening to the Sheriff's words on a car radio, he bounded back to the house to find his wife. When he walked in, Shirley was sitting completely still on the couch in front of the television, her face numb with shock. Rick slipped his arms around his wife in a comforting embrace then took her arm and gently led her into their bedroom. There, the emotion released, and the hurt flowed uninhibited.

For almost an hour, Shirley wept in her husband's arms, giant sobs racking through her. All those mornings she stood at the window, thinking of those babies. All the times she'd stood up for Susan, defended her, believed in her.

The betrayal, the anger, the bitterness. It exploded from deep within Shirley McCloud.

"I can't believe this woman duped me," she

wept. "I'll never help anyone again. I'll never do this again. Never, never."

She felt like a child, sobbing uncontrollably, so helpless and vulnerable in her husband's arms. When she finally reappeared in the den, her aunt and uncle sat her down on the couch, trying to find words of comfort they knew did not exist.

Suddenly, the side door flew open and a woman, a stranger who was watching events unfold from the road by John D. Long Lake, burst into the McCloud's family room.

"She done it! She done it!" the woman screamed.

Shirley's patience was all but gone.

"Who is this?" she snapped to her family, her voice rising. "Get this woman out of my house right now."

Shirley's uncle jumped up and led the woman out.

It was not the last interruption of the night. A short time later a woman appeared at the side door, asking to use the phone.

Shirley just glared. The woman, she knew, was a local television reporter. Shirley McCloud was no fool. She knew the woman was more interested in getting Shirley's reaction to Susan's confession than in making any phone calls.

"You're not using the phone here," she said firmly. "Don't you have one, anyway?"

The woman fumbled for an answer. Shirley's husband, she explained, had said she could use their phone in the house. Shirley stayed firm. After she left, Shirley rolled her eyes. Her husband, she thought, was too trusting, too nice.

"That woman just wanted to get inside my house," she fumed to Rick a few minutes later. Later that week, Shirley was proved right. The television reporter later filmed a stand-up segment for the evening news in front of the McCloud house.

"To say the least," the woman said on the air, her voice sympathetic, "Mrs. McCloud is very distraught."

In Bend, Oregon, Jeanne Boylan heard the news from a CBS producer. The man had called her to discuss a case and casually mentioned the rumor that Susan Smith had confessed to murder. Jeanne quickly told him she'd get back to him, and hung up. She paged Marc Klaas. As she punched in her number and waited, she wondered if he'd heard the rumors.

He had.

When the phone rang and she picked it up. Marc didn't even wait for her to speak.

"Jeanne, she killed them, didn't she?" he said.

"Marc, I don't know," she answered.

Just then, her call waiting beeped.

"Hold on a minute," she said.

A minute later, Jeanne was back. It had been the CBS producer. He told her that Sheriff Wells had just come on the news and confirmed it.

"Marc, it's true," Jeanne said, breaking into tears. "She's confessed."

Marc and Jeanne shared their sorrow on the telephone. When Marc hung up, the ache that consumed him had an all-too-familiar feel. Beyond all the sorrow, he had been so angered by his daughter's death. Polly had been home the night she was kidnapped and murdered, home in her own bedroom, her mother asleep in the next room. Richard Allen Davis had stepped in through the back door and ruptured so many lives in an instant.

Polly should have been safe, he thought again. And what, now, of Michael and Alex Smith? They, too, should have been safe. Their story was even more impossible to comprehend.

Marc asked himself every day what kind of world makes a monster like the one who killed his daughter. He thought about Susan Smith. Was she a Richard Allen Davis? He always knew that something wasn't right in Union, South Carolina. But never did he think that a mother could do what Susan Smith had apparently done.

All the images flashed before him. Polly, those little boys, all the missing children, all the heartbroken faces of their parents. That afternoon,

Marc waited anxiously for his wife Violet to return from work.

She alone would know precisely how he felt.

WBCU's gospel show host Carlisle Henderson also learned the news by phone. A reporter called him just before Wells made his statement. When she told him what she'd heard, he called out, "Georgia, pick up the telephone!"

His wife reached for the phone in the kitchen. With both Hendersons on the phone, the reporter explained what she had learned. "I feel like I'm dreaming," Carlisle said. "Would you please repeat this?"

He began to cry, his breath coming in short gasps.

"Mr. Henderson," the reporter said, pausing. "Are you laughing?"

Carlisle Henderson's sobs grew louder. "No," he moaned. "I'm not laughing. I don't believe it. I just don't believe it."

After watching Sheriff Wells appearance on television, Carlisle told his wife that he had the same feeling he'd had that day in November 1963 when he learned President Kennedy had been assassinated in Dallas. He had picked up the phone and an operator had come on to ask him what number he wanted. Tearfully, he'd told the operator the President was dead. And the operator, too, had begun to cry.

That night, and for many nights afterward,

Carlisle relied on the only source of comfort he knew. He said prayers for the Russell and the Smith families. He asked the Lord to heal the broken heart of his community.

And then, Carlisle prayed for Susan. *That girl just wasn't in her right mind,* he thought. *I feel like her mind snapped. Just snapped.*

He decided he would tell the community of Union about that the very next day, on his gospel radio show. He would tell, Susan, too, in case she was listening.

God, he believed, had already forgiven Susan. God loved her, and so Carlisle Henderson did, too. But that night, Carlisle Henderson shed tears for the little boys he knew were at last with God.

He thought about how when he moved to Union in the early 1950s he had run a local funeral home. Surrounded daily by the grief of families and friends who had lost loved ones, Carlisle had come to believe that death was not something to be mourned with tears and wails. He found a way to trust that God knew what He was doing.

But his tears fell for Michael and Alex Smith. And for the young woman whose smile he could still picture.

There were no tears from Gilliam Edwards that night, there was only anger. Edwards was among the townspeople who'd gathered on East

Main Street to hear Sheriff Wells's statement and he was consumed with rage when his theory that Susan Smith had made up the story of a black carjacker was officially confirmed. Moments after the sheriff had gone back inside his office, the fifty-three-year-old black man began to shout. "It's always a black man, always a black man. It's time for us to stand up like men and women and stop the whites from accusing us of hideous crimes that they commit against themselves and they have committed against us for 484 years."

Gilliam kept going. Emotions were running high as it was. His soared.

"What kind of people accuse defenseless people?" he thundered. "We black people are totally defenseless. We shouldn't accept that no more. We got to fight back. We don't stand up for ourselves."

Some in the crowd tried to shout him down, but most paid little attention. Now, in the wake of the news about the Smith boys, it hardly seemed the time to debate racial injustices.

The reporters, though, knew a news story when they heard it. And this sounded like a good one: Susan Smith's shocking admission of murder splits a community along racial lines. The evidence was right there on Main Street, in the contentious words of Gilliam Edwards.

The journalists surrounded him, thrusting microphones before the factory worker and father of seven. Gilliam was only too happy to continue his rampage. His wife and children didn't listen anymore, his friends told him he was too radical, that he talked too much.

But that night, as hundreds wept in the streets of Union, South Carolina, Gilliam Edwards had at last found his forum. If the timing didn't suit anyone else, that was just too bad.

Gilliam Edwards would not stop now. There had been no black man, no nameless, faceless carjacker spiriting away the little white boys in the dark of night, he thundered. And he'd known it all along. No brother of his had made off with those white children. People like Susan Smith, people who didn't know what it was like to be a black man in a small Southern town, who wanted to blame him for their horrible deeds, they took no responsibility, only shifted blame.

"We ain't got no army," he told reporters earnestly. "We ain't got no police. And yet we are being depicted and used as a political statement. Anything that we learn as criminals, we learned it from the white people. We didn't come here from Africa as criminals. We came here as farmers. In Africa we didn't have no such word for criminal, or jail, or hate, or racism. All that was taught to us since we been here."

He told them his motto. It was simple and honest. "If you wrong me, I got a right to wrong you back," he said. "So right me, and I'll right you back."

Gilliam's angry discourse was broadcast around the nation. In the days to come, newspapers would run editorials lashing out at a nation so quick to believe blacks were so responsible for society's ills.

It would recall the story of Charles Stuart, the Boston man who shot and killed his pregnant wife in a parked car and then frantically called 911 to report that he and his wife had been attacked by a black man. In his tortured conversation with the dispatcher, later broadcast again and again across the nation, Stuart said a young black man with a gun had accosted them after they had taken a wrong turn on their way home from a Lamaze childbirth class at Boston's Brigham and Women's Hospital. The black man, he'd said, had demanded his wallet and his wife's purse, and then shot her in the head and him in the stomach to cover up the crime.

In the coming days, the Boston police aggressively questioned dozens of black men in the largely black neighborhood of Roxbury. But even as they did so, detectives gradually became suspicious of Stuart's story. Fearing the truth was about to emerge, Stuart committed suicide, jumping off a bridge.

Outraged by police treatment of blacks during the investigation, Boston's African-American leaders staged angry protest rallies, demanding an apology from city officials and even the resignation of some top police brass.

But while Gilliam Edwards's rage made headlines, the nation soon discovered that he was not speaking for the majority of Union's black population. During their investigation, two of Sheriff Wells's deputies had, in fact, spoken to several black men in Union about the reported carjacking, and even brought two into headquarters for questioning. Nonetheless, both men would later say they were treated respectfully by the officers, and that they held no grudge against the sheriff's department.

From the pulpits of the town's black churches, the community's ministers preached a message of healing not division. The night after Susan's confession, the people of Union staged a town meeting to pledge their desire for unity in the face of this tragedy. They followed it with a prayer vigil, asking the Lord to bring peace and harmony to their heartbroken community.

More than a hundred blacks and whites attended the vigil, hoping to find comfort as well as send a message to the nation that their city was not bitterly divided on racial lines. Indeed, they said, many of the lines that had been drawn in the centuries of the old South had, in fact, blurred in the aftermath of the Smith tragedy.

16

The SLED helicopter returned Sheriff Howard Wells to John D. Long Lake at seven P.M. Though the sun had already set, the area, packed with law enforcement agents, was awash in light, thanks to the beams of the tall flood lights set up along the shore.

In one corner, a team of forensic experts talked quietly with William Holcombe, the Union County Coroner. The 34-year-old Holcombe also headed the city's largest funeral home, Holcombe's, a forty-five-year-old business begun by Holcombe's grandfather. In small southern towns, it isn't uncommon for county coroners to also run funeral homes. Holcombe had been elected coroner four years earlier and was expected to be reelected at the following week's election.

In his role as funeral director, Holcombe had come to know the Smith family well. He had arranged the wake and burial for David's brother Danny three years earlier. Now, in his role as county coroner, he was preparing himself to deal with another Smith family tragedy.

Wildlife department divers Morrow, Mitchum, Jackson and Robert Stuckey of Sumter, had been waiting for Wells's return to begin recovery of the sunken Mazda. The sheriff had wanted to be on hand when the Smith boys were finally pulled from their watery grave. With the sheriff's arrival, they could resume their grim assignment. The four men headed out to the marker, 100 feet from shore. They carried with them a thirty-foot cable and chain that was attached to a tow truck parked on the shore.

At one point, perched on the edge of the small boat, Francis Mitchum gazed at the shore, clearly upset. He kept thinking how close they'd come to finding the car on one of the earlier dives. He told Jackson they'd probably come within ten to fifteen feet the last time.

But as seasoned as they were, the divers never expected a car would have floated nearly 100 feet from the water's edge. That, and the poor visibility in the murky lake water, had caused them to give up too soon.

"If we made one more pass," Mitchum told Jackson, "we would have found it."

When they reached the marker, Francis Mitchum and Steve Morrow dove down the eighteen feet to the bottom of the lake and attached the chain to the frame of the Mazda. The windshield of the muddy car had cracked, not surprising given its nine days of temperature change and water pressure at the lake's silty bottom.

When the cable and chains were in place, Mitchum and Morrow signaled Curtis Jackson, who had remained in the small boat. It was his responsibility to keep the law-enforcement agents on land aware of what was going on in the lake. When Mitchum and Morrow were ready, Jackson motioned to the driver of the wrecker to pull.

As the Mazda was slowly dragged up from its muddy resting place, Steve Morrow and Francis Mitchum hung along to the car's sides. It was important that they stay with the vehicle to ensure doors or windows didn't fly open accidentally.

It took about forty-five minutes for the wrecker to pull the car through the mud along the lake bottom and into shallow water. Once it hit shallow water, the wrecker pulled the car sharply, flipping it right-side up.

"We all saw what we saw," Sheriff Wells would later tell reporters, tightly. "We had a plan, the plan was carried out, and everyone there saw what was there."

He didn't say the men wept that night, as the bodies of Michael and Alexander Smith were unbuckled from their carseats and carried out. But they did, unashamedly. It was a scene that will not fade from the memories of the fifty or so men who were there for many years to come.

The children's bodies were placed in a waiting ambulance, which traveled through the night to the University of South Carolina Medical Center in Charleston. An autopsy performed early the next day confirmed that the boys had been alive when their mother sent them into the lake, and that they had drowned as the car submerged.

When his assignment was over, Steve Morrow did not linger at the lake. He said good-bye to his fellow divers and shook hands with Howard Wells. Then, he got into his van and drove directly home.

His wife, Lorrie, thirty, was waiting up for him. Like everyone else, she had heard about the confession. She had picked up their four-year-old son, Mac, from his day-care center in Union, and come home to find both the van and her husband gone. And so she understood.

She hugged him and for a few minutes, they talked. It seemed to Steve Morrow that there wasn't much to say, not tonight at least. Brushing away tears, Morrow opened the door to Mac's room, just a crack. He could hear the regular breathing of his only child. He saw the covers askew, as Mac had shifted position in his sleep.

Steve Morrow sat on his son's bed, and

stroked the child's hair. He didn't know how long he remained there, motionless, watching his baby sleep. Then, Steve Morrow thought of the only thing in the world that would comfort him right now. He gently moved Mac to make room, and settled down next to him.

He wrapped his arms around his son. And eventually, he, too, slept.

Howard Wells arrived home around midnight. Wanda and her friends from the bank had spent a few hours together after work, talking and crying. Wanda had had a flat tire, so one of her friends had driven her home. The two women had talked for a while about the tragedy.

"I guess you've heard what's happened," Howard Wells said to his wife.

"I heard when you announced it at the news conference," Wanda said. "But I heard it on the radio before. Plus, I think the Associated Press had released some information before that they thought there was going to be a confession and it was thought to be the mother."

Wells shook his head in amazement. "You've got to be kidding," he said.

"No, I'm not kidding."

Howard Wells walked to his blue recliner. He leaned back and stared at the ceiling. He did not say anything else. And Wanda didn't ask.

[17]

The day after the world learned of the deaths of Michael and Alex Smith, J. Cary Findlay issued a stern warning to his staff, posted in the hallways: talk to the press about Susan Smith or Tom Findlay, and be fired. To keep curiosity seekers and reporters out, Findlay hired guards at his estate, and to patrol the entrances to Conso. Findlay also hired an attorney for his son, who issued a letter from Tom. It read:

> I am devastated by this tragedy. I cooperated and have been cooperating with the legal authorities since last week in the disappearance of Susan Smith's children. The only reason I am coming forward to issue this statement now is because of the continuing inaccurate reports of my relationship with Smith.

I did have a relationship with Ms. Smith and on October 18 I told her that I was terminating that relationship for a number of reasons and gave her a copy of a letter to that effect, a letter which I gave to the authorities early in this investigation. One of the reasons for my termination of the relationship was that I was not ready to assume the important responsibilities of being a father.

However, that was far from the only reason for terminating the relationship and certainly was not the most important. At no time did I suggest to Ms. Smith that her children were the only obstacle in any potential relationship with her.

I know nothing about what happened that night or why it happened.

I intend to continue cooperating with the law-enforcement authorities in their investigation and I share in the grief of this community in the loss of the two children. I will make no further statements.

Earlier that day, a well-dressed man stood outside of Joyce Flowers & Gifts on Main Street in downtown Union, waiting patiently for it to open.

Shortly after eight A.M., Paul Patrick, Joyce's husband, arrived. He greeted the stranger, surprised to find him waiting. Patrick fumbled with a sizable collection of keys, and unlocked the door.

The man told him he wanted to send flowers in memory of the Smith children.

"I was coming through town," he explained to Patrick. "I felt like I had to do something."

Patrick nodded.

"What are you looking for?" he asked.

The man requested a large cross made of blue and white carnations with a banner that read, "We love you." He filled out a card and paid for his purchase.

"Could you take it down to the lake?" he asked.

Patrick wasn't sure he'd heard correctly.

"To where?" he said.

"The lake," the man replied. "I thought that would be appropriate."

"What do you mean? Whereabouts?"

"Just set it on the ground."

Patrick told him he would. Later that morning, the first flowers made their way to the edge of John D. Long Lake. Within days, flowers covered the boat ramp and the surrounding grass. The brick-and-concrete plaque at the rim of the parking lot that read "John D. Long Lake. Named by the General Assembly of S.C. for John D. Long, 1901–1967. Senator, Sportsman, Friend," would ultimately be entirely shrouded with notes and poems, children's drawings, toys, and balloons.

By mid-morning on Friday November 4, the orders to Joyce florist were coming in rapidly. They arrived from mourners all over the United States, and even from Canada and Mexico. In all, more than 700 callers had flowers sent to the lake, the church or the cemetery in memory of the murdered boys.

Almost none of the callers had ever met Michael or Alex Smith, and most didn't even know the family. One caller ordered two crosses and requested that they be placed on either side of the casket. Another spent $275 for an arrangement of red flowers shaped like a heart and decorated with two teddy bears.

During the days after the boys' bodies were discovered, Patrick's wife, Joyce, often stood by the teletype, watching the orders as they came in. She'd read the messages people had asked to have sent along with their flowers. More than once, Patrick saw his wife cry at the teletype machine.

Every few hours, Patrick and his wife called wholesalers, ordering more flowers, more plants.

Earlier that morning, Lisa Caveny, an FTD representative had called the Patricks to warn them to expect a deluge of orders. The international flower delivery service was channeling requests to them from around the world. "Do you know what you're in for?" Lisa asked. "It's going to be like catching five gallons in a coffee cup."

Patrick told her they could handle it. After all, they'd been in business for thirty years. Nonetheless, they were stunned by the volume. By noon, the couple had called their daughter and niece in to help answer phones.

By 2:00 P.M., Patrick told the women to tell anyone else who called that they could no longer do custom designs—no more teddy bears, hearts, or crosses.

"No more special stuff," he said. "Tell everybody it's open orders."

An hour later, he told reporters to leave the store. They'd been coming in all day, asking questions, poking around. "You can't talk to them," he'd say as they continued to try to pester his daughter and niece for details about the orders coming in.

Finally, he kicked them out. "All of you guys got to go," he said. "Now."

As he worked, Patrick thought back to the times he'd spoken to Susan Smith on the phone. Ever since she had begun working at Conso in 1993, she'd frequently called in company orders, buying elaborate arrangements to display in the Conso lobby or to decorate tables at special events. He remembered how polite and soft spoken she sounded, that light Southern drawl.

During the week the search was on, Patrick

had fielded several calls from people who wanted to send flowers to Susan and the Russell family. The requests had made him uncomfortable, and he'd told the callers so.

"I think it's a little premature," he'd always say.

But the customers always insisted. They said they were friends of Susan's or co-workers. They wanted to show their concern, and to tell the family their prayers were with them.

Patrick learned of the children's death from patrons at a Rock Hill mall where he had been shopping with his daughter and grandson. Once a week, when his wife went to visit her mother, Patrick drove about twenty minutes to his daughter's house to spend the evening with her.

Although Susan's confession stunned Patrick, he reminded his family that he'd always said her story wasn't true. He'd grown up in a house near the corner of Monarch School Drive and Highway 149. He knew the Monarch red light. He knew the area. He just couldn't picture how a man could jump in anybody's car, unseen.

As the days passed he'd watched Shirley McCloud on television, describing Susan's demeanor that night, how nobody could have faked that, but it still didn't convince him.

* * *

Toward the end of the day on Friday, an older woman called in a $20 order to Joyce's florists. Patrick took her information.

The woman said she wanted the arrangement sent to the church. Then, there was a pause.

"How do I know you'll actually send it there?" she asked.

Patrick's temper rose. "Lady, I got two kids, two grandkids. I couldn't sleep at night if I did that. Look, why don't we forget it. Let's just forget the order."

"No, no," the woman interrupted. "It's fine."

But it was too late. "Well, no," Patrick said brusquely. "I'm cancelling your order."

And he did.

By 10 P.M. that night, Patrick was exhausted. His wife, Joyce, and their daughter and niece had joined him in the back of the shop, designing and making flower arrangements for the next day's deliveries. At last the phones had stopped ringing, the teletype machine was quiet.

But the women had been talking nonstop for hours, and it was starting to get to him. He'd been trying to ignore them but it grew harder as time passed.

The women spoke wistfully of the children, those innocent little faces they'd seen in the newspaper and on TV. They wondered aloud about the boys' last moments, about the fateful car trip and the cold water in the lake.

Patrick kept warning them to stop. "Listen, I can't take no more of this," he snapped. "Please, please stop talking about that."

For a few minutes the women would fall silent, wrapping flowers and attaching bows. But then someone would start again. How horrible, how unforgiveable, what she did. Imagine. A mother, blessed with children. Anyone would have taken those little boys. Anyone.

Finally, Patrick tossed his work aside.

"Hell, I'm getting out of here," he barked.

His wife, Joyce, reached for his hand, concerned. She knew how much the deaths of those children hurt.

"You go on, then," she said kindly. "Go home."

Patrick drove through the deserted streets of Union. At home, he reached for a bottle of Chivas. He rarely drank, but that night, Paul Patrick poured a half glass and downed it. He went to bed and lay there for hours, unable to sleep.

At three A.M., he threw off the covers, got dressed and returned to the store.

At six o'clock Saturday morning, Patrick stepped outside the store to meet the first truckload of extra flowers he'd ordered from the wholesaler. By nine, a steady stream of out-of-town visitors had begun dropping by the shop to pick up bouquets of flowers to bring to the lake. All day, Patrick's wife stopped working when visitors asked for directions to John D. Long Lake. She'd pull out paper and pen, and painstakingly draw a map: Take East Main Street straight out until it becomes Highway 49. Pass the red light at the intersection of Highway 49 and Monarch School Drive and in a few miles, go over Meng Creek. Pass over Big Brown's Creek and Little Brown's Creek and a few miles out, turn left at the John D. Long Lake sign.

It was really quite simple, she'd explain.

Joyce Patrick also promised a handful of callers that she would mail them newspaper clippings about the children's funeral, and agreed to send photographs of several callers' flower arrangements once things had settled down. She told the callers to call back if they hadn't received their pictures soon. "Now I might forget," she warned them. "So be sure and call me to remind me."

That day, her husband took a break and looked around at all the activity in his shop.

It's like a big holiday but nobody's happy, he thought sadly.

18

On Thursday night November 3, the night police recovered Michael and Alex's bodies from the bottom of John D. Long Lake, David Smith finally left the home of his wife's parents and headed back to his two-bedroom apartment on Lakeside Drive. He had barely spent any time there in the nine days his sons were missing. His father and stepmother went with him, and a little later, his sister, Becky, and some of his friends from Winn-Dixie stopped by, too.

About nine P.M., Becky's estranged husband, Wallace Tucker, knocked timidly on the apartment's front door. He'd gotten off work at Helig-Meyers furniture store, where he drove a delivery truck, around six o'clock, about the time word was spreading of Susan Smith's arrest and the fate of her children.

Wallace had thought about it for a while, and then decided to stop by David's. He'd always liked his brother-in-law. These days, with his marriage to Becky on the rocks, he didn't see him often. But they bumped into each other now and again, and Wallace felt a familial bond.

David met Wallace at the door and the young men embraced. David motioned for Wallace to follow him, and they went into David's bedroom to talk. Wallace tried not to notice the other bedroom, replete with toys, a crib, and a small bed.

Wallace told David that he was sorry he hadn't stopped by the Russell house during the week the boys were missing. He said he felt funny—he was black, and, after all, there was all this talk about a black carjacker. It made him a little queasy.

"I'd be there, the only black guy . . . I thought they'd look at me funny, know what I mean?" he said.

"I understand," David told him. "I'm sorry you didn't feel comfortable."

Sitting on the edge of his bed, David Smith told his brother-in-law that he felt nothing, just a hollowness, an empty space inside.

"It might seem strange that I'm not crying," he said. "I'm just in a deep, heavy shock. It still hasn't hit me that my babies are gone, that my wife killed our children."

Wallace nodded. He wasn't sure what to say.

"Were you with her when she confessed?" he asked.

"No," David answered. Over the course of the investigation, he explained, the sheriff and FBI had taken them to different places around town to talk. They'd been talking to Susan a lot but he hadn't known they were meeting with her that day.

"That day, she left and she said she was going to take a letter somewhere," David told Wallace. "After two hours, I figured something's wrong."

Wallace asked David if David's mother was on her way to Union. He said she was. Barbara Benson was expected to get into town around eleven P.M. Shortly after Sheriff Wells left the Russell home, David had called her at home in Surf City. Sobbing uncontrollably, he tried to tell her what the sheriff had said. Barbara Benson couldn't quite make out her son's voice. Then she heard him say the words she had been dreading: "Sheriff Wells just confirmed it. Susan confessed. She killed the children."

Sitting in his bedroom that night, David told Wallace what a complete shock it had been to learn that Susan had murdered their sons. "I believed her," he said, shaking his head. "I believed her right until the end."

David got up and picked up a framed photograph atop his bureau. It was taken before Alex was born so it was just David, Susan, and Michael, all smiling.

"Susan," David said, staring at the photo.

"How could you do it? How could you kill our little boy?"

David's eyes were dry, but the moment was too much for Wallace. The young man brushed away tears.

David turned to his friend. "I would have gladly taken them," he told Wallace. "If it was too much for her, I would have taken them."

Wallace knew that was true. In the three years he'd been married to David's sister, he'd seen how close David was to his boys. He remembered how David talked about fixing a room for the boys in his new apartment, how he wanted to make sure they felt the apartment was their home, too. Wallace thought back to the last time he'd seen his nephews, when he'd bumped into Susan, David and the children at the Union Agricultural Fair a few weeks earlier.

He could still picture the little family: David carrying Alex, Susan holding Michael's hand.

Before Wallace left, David told him that officials had asked him to come down to the Holcombe funeral home the next day to identify the bodies of his children.

Wallace did not say anything. Later, he talked to Becky about it on the steps outside David's apartment.

"If it was me, I wouldn't do it," he said.

Becky was surprised.

"You wouldn't want to see your kids one last time?"

Wallace shrugged. Perhaps he would, if he was in David's place. He felt lucky he wasn't.

Minutes after learning that Susan had confessed to killing her children, Bev Russell called the home of Reverend Mark Long, the pastor of Buffalo United Methodist church. Long's wife answered. She explained that her husband wasn't home—he'd already left for Union City Hall where he was to meet other local ministers and make their planned public appeal to the carjacker.

Once Margaret Long heard the news she immediately drove to Union. By the time she'd parked and hurried to the courthouse Sheriff Wells's statement to the media had ended. Margaret Long pushed through the crowd still milling along Main Street. She scanned the sea of troubled faces for her husband. She finally found him, talking privately with several other pastors.

She gently tugged at his sleeve. "You need to go to the Russell house," she told her husband. "They need you."

She explained about the phone call from Bev Russell. Reverend Long left immediately for the Russell house; his wife joined him there minutes later.

The Longs stayed at the Russell house from seven o'clock that night until almost ten. The minister led the family in prayers. Everyone—

Linda and Bev, David, Scotty and Wendy Vaughan, and other family and friends—wept unabashedly.

That night, the coroner, William Holcombe, called and spoke to David. He asked the young man what funeral home he wanted to use.

The answer was obvious, but Holcombe had to ask.

"We'd like Holcombe," David said.

They agreed to meet the following day. Then, David Smith and his in-laws asked Long to perform the funeral service for Michael and Alex at Buffalo United Methodist. The children had attended Sunday School there. It seemed the right place to say their good-byes.

At noon on Friday, November 5, David, his parents, Bev and Linda, and Scotty and Wendy Vaughan met with Holcombe for about an hour and a half. Through tears, the family of Michael and Alex Smith outlined how they wanted to tell their boys good-bye. They asked Holcombe to lay the boys out together, in a white casket with gold trim and set up a time for visitation at the funeral home for the next evening, from seven until nine. The casket, they insisted, would remain closed.

The funeral, to be held the following day, would begin at 2:00 P.M. at Buffalo United Methodist Church, with four local ministers officiating. The Rev. Mark Long, they said, had been asked to offer the final eulogy. Afterward, the boys would be buried in the cemetery behind Bogansville United Methodist Church, right next to the grave of Danny Smith, David's older brother and the children's uncle.

"We want it dignified and respectful," one family member told Holcombe. "Please give it reverence."

William Holcombe nodded. Speaking in a soft voice, he assured the family that Holcombe Funeral Home would provide a sensitive and comforting atmosphere for their family and friends in their time of need.

The family then discussed the media. They realized that after the extensive national attention the nine-day search for the children had received, they had to expect an onslaught of reporters and camera crews as they laid their boys to rest. They did not want any photographers permitted at the visitation or at the funeral and only one pool photographer at the burial.

Later, Bev Russell and Rev. Long proposed an audio feed of the funeral so that mourners who could not get into the church because of space limitations could listen to the service outside. That seemed to appease the journalists, who called Buffalo United Methodist Church relentlessly about arrangements for the Sunday service.

* * *

The Rev. Mark Long normally prepared a brief outline for his Sunday morning sermons, then spent the day before the service jotting notes and checking Bible verses.

But when it came to offering a eulogy for two little boys whose death had touched so many people, the minister knew that the words would come freely from his heart. In the day he had to prepare for the service, his mind raced with all the things he wanted to say, the words he imagined would comfort the family and bring them a measure of peace.

He decided he would not discuss Susan and forgiveness. That message, he believed, was best saved for another time.

Rev. Long made up his mind to use a text from the Old Testament's second book of Samuel, to tell the story of how King David reacted to the death of his infant son. He also wanted to quote from Psalm Eighty-eight, a psalm of pain and agony, of questioning the faithfulness of God. From there, he would lead mourners to the comfort of the Twenty-third Psalm and its message of hope and faith, that the Lord would be with them always.

It was his purpose, the reverend believed, to reassure the family of Michael and Alex Smith, and all others who shared their grief that while the world is sometimes a place of great pain and tragedy, that does not mean that God is not there. It does not mean God does not care.

* * *

The day after he met with the family at the Russell house, Long called the other three ministers the family had asked to participate in the funeral service. He gave them each a suggestion of what topics to focus on.

The Reverend Joe Bridges, Interim Minister of the Tabernacle Baptist Church, he had decided, would speak first, about Jesus and his special love for children. Rev. Doug Gilliland of Bogansville United Methodist Church would lead the congregation in the Lord's Prayer. Rev. Bob Cato would talk about faith.

On Saturday evening, Resident Bishop of the South Carolina Conference United Methodist Churches Joseph Bethea called .Rev. Long at home. He told him that he would like to attend the funeral, not to participate, but to give him support. Rev. Long thanked his superior and told him he appreciated it.

When he hung up, the minister made a mental note to make sure the bishop had a seat.

Visitors began showing up at Holcombe Funeral Home at ten A.M. Saturday, even though the visitation was not scheduled to begin until seven that night. In all, more than 1,000 people came through that night, signing the registry, leaving flowers and mass cards. Some 700 gifts of flowers were delivered, including one from President Bill Clinton.

Throughout the visitation, a tearful David Smith hugged hundreds of people and talked quietly with friends. At one point, David pulled aside his grandfather, Jim Martin, who had flown in from California for the funeral, and asked him not to speak badly of Susan. Martin had been approached by reporters, and David was concerned about what he might say.

"Don't trash Susan," David said to him quietly.

Despite the horror of what she had done, Susan was still his children's mother.

[19]

Two nights earlier, he had prayed with the weeping families of Michael and Alex Smith, but Rev. Mark Long's own tears did not flow until 1:30 A.M. Sunday, about twelve hours before the funeral. He woke up crying, suddenly feeling tremendous pressure about his eulogy for the boys. He knew, too, that he had to get through his regular Sunday service at eleven. Right now, all he could think of was the funeral.

What if he couldn't summon the right words?

His wife, Margaret, held him as he talked out his anxieties.

"I need to get back to the eleven A.M. service," he kept saying. "I need to focus on the eleven."

Eventually, the minister calmed down. He asked God to give him the message to comfort all those who would listen to him the next day.

* * *

At the end of the eleven A.M. service, Long reminded his congregation that many, many strangers would turn up at their church that day and would likely fill the pews quickly. Any one resolved to find a seat for a funeral would be wise to simply remain in their seats. Holcombe Funeral Home had planned to rope off the first sixteen rows for the families of the two boys. The back row would be reserved for the press.

By one o'clock the casket carrying the bodies of Michael and Alex Smith arrived from the funeral home and was placed near the altar.

Just before the funeral was set to begin, a reporter managed to corner Sheriff Wells, who was standing at the back of the church. The reporter asked Wells about the latest bombshell to break in the case: a report in *Newsweek* magazine that quoted an unnamed source saying Susan Smith had told investigators that she had seen her son Michael flail about in his car seat as the car sank.

Wells brushed it off. "That's the most preposterous thing I've ever heard," he said.

Outside, Barbara Benson, David's mother, stood alone on the church steps. A Jehovah's Witness, Benson does not believe in churches and had rejected the offer to sit inside with the family. She stood outside, uninterested in what anyone else thought about her decision. She had previously refused to enter the church in

Bogansville where funeral services were held for her son, Danny, three years earlier.

Barbara had loved Danny, just as she loved her grandchildren. Her religious beliefs didn't change that. Whether she stood outside or sat inside, her sorrow was great.

The funeral for Michael and Alexander Smith began with the mournful sounds of the church organ. The congregation joined together for the first hymn, "Praise to the Lord, the Almighty."

David, wearing a navy blue suit and dark red tie, wept throughout the hour-long service.

Rev. Doug Gilliland opened with these words:

"O God, we who have assembled here along with thousands across our state and nation cry out to you in our hour of need. Come, Holy Comforter, deliver us from the devastation, the brokenheartedness that we feel in the loss of little Michael and Alex Smith."

"Help this family and community, O God, to overcome such tragedy. Help us to know within the depth of our hearts that you hear our plea and have mercy upon us."

Speaking to the mourners, Rev. Gilliland asked them to stand. "Will you join me in the prayer that Jesus taught his disciples," he said.

Solemnly, hundreds of voices, inside and outside the church, began reciting the Lord's Prayer. Then the crowd prayed silently as the children's hymn "Jesus Loves Me" was tapped out on the organ.

The next minister to speak was Joe Bridges.

"I want to say this to all of you who have gathered here and especially the family, that God loves you and cares about you. Just because you've gone through the deep waters and just because the tears come so easily, and they do, to all of our eyes, does not mean that God does not care and does not love you.

"He loves you and cares for you and Michael and Alex have just gone home to be with the Lord. I know that because we miss them. Sometimes God takes the most precious jewels in life to give them back to us in eternity where we never lose them. We cannot bring them back but we can go and be with them . . ."

Silence fell again. The organ rang out with the sounds of "Away in a Manger."

Rev. Bob Cato was next. He looked directly at the members of the Smith family, leaning on each other, wracked with grief. He faced the congregation and his voice resonated through the church.

"On Tuesday night," he began, "David and his family and friends were in my home and one of the folks in the circle of friends said this: 'We want the boys home.' "

There was a pause. Rev. Cato looked out into the sea of sorrowful faces.

"They're home," he repeated. "They're home where they belong. They're home. They're home where there's no more pain, no more turmoil, no more anguish, no more people screaming across the streets at each other trying to get a word in edgewise . . .

"Someone asked me about what had happened in our little town. He said, 'Preacher, what do you think God's thinking right now?' And I didn't have an answer. And this person, who is not a believer, said, 'Preacher, do you know what God is like?'

"And I said, 'I know some things from his word, his Bible.' And then he asked me this, and it sounds so silly, maybe ludicrous. 'Have you ever seen God?' And I replied 'No, I have never seen the face of God but I've seen the face of his children.'

"I've never seen God's robe, but I know that I will wear it one day. I've never seen the feet of God but I have walked alongside some of his children and adults who have lost their precious children.

"In short, I have not seen God but I have seen his handiwork. And Michael and Alex were his handiwork. And now, they see God.

"I would rather think of them this afternoon as sitting in his lap. I think Michael would be on one knee, Alex on the other. And what would God say to them? Something like this: 'Kids, do you see all the people down there? They love you, but not near as much as I love you.'

"So if they're home, where does that leave us?

That leaves us right here in a little town with all the world watching us today. The question is, how do we cope?

"Well, we cope the same way that we always have. Knowing that we are not in control of things. We cope in faith in God. In a faith in a God that never makes mistakes . . ."

The Reverend Cato told a story about a man standing on one side of Niagara Falls. Stretched across was a cable. The man walked back and forth across the cable and onlookers cheered and clapped. Then, he took a wheelbarrow and pushed it across.

When he returned he asked the people if they believed he could place someone in the wheelbarrow and push it across the great falls. The people, Cato told the mourners, cheered.

"Then," he said, "he asked this question: 'Who will step forward now and get in the wheelbarrow and let me push you across?' And nobody would step forward."

Cato paused.

"Folks, I think it's time for the people of this family, and the people of Union County and the people of the state of South Carolina and America and the world to get in God's wheelbarrow and see what he can do," he told them, his voice strong. "We've got to have faith. We've got to have faith."

* * *

A hush came over the church as Reverend Long stepped up to the pulpit. Behind him, in the choir loft, sat United Methodist Bishop Joseph Bethea. He'd gotten the only seat left in the church.

Reverend Long opened with the story he had planned to tell from the start: he told the mourners about King David, how God had willed his infant son to die, and how in the days before the child's death, David had wept and prayed as the baby grew sicker.

David, the minister said, had refused food. He didn't wash or change clothes.

And then the baby died. David's aides, Reverend Long said, were afraid to tell him, but David heard them whispering and asked if the baby was dead. They told him he was.

David got up. He prayed. Then he washed himself, changed clothes and ate.

Said Long, "His aides were amazed. 'We don't understand you,' they said. 'While the baby was still living you wept and refused to eat but now that the baby is dead you've stopped your mourning and are eating again.'

"David replied, 'I have fasted and wept while the child was alive. For I said perhaps the Lord will be gracious to me and let the child live. But why should I fast when he is dead? Can I bring him back again? I shall go to him but he shall not return to me.' David prayed and prayed and the baby died. God had willed for this child to die.

"And David was wondering, 'Why? Why did this have to happen?' Have any of you ever asked that question, 'Why?' Why does this have to be? In some ways we come to ask the same question. Some of us come in a sense of anger and cry, 'Why does God allow this to happen?'

"And we search for answers."

Reverend Long spoke of the Twenty-third Psalm. He said it was read at every funeral service, and that it was meant to give comfort and cheer. He questioned whether it did.

The minister told the people that he had found a way where it did, a way to interpret to the Psalm, so that it made sense. He told them about the Eighty-eighth Psalm, a psalm of anguish and pain.

"I can see David at that moment when he's on his face before God and all he hears is nothing," Long said, his voice echoing through the church. "He cries out to God, 'Hear me!' and God doesn't answer. All David hears is silence. At that moment in time I think that David remembers the Eighty-eighth Psalm."

"Hear the psalm. Here the pain within it, the questioning, the doubt, the anguish. Hear the trust. 'Oh, Jehovah, God of my salvation. I have wept before you day and night. Now hear my prayers. Oh, listen to my cry, for my life is full of troubles and death draws near.

" 'They say my life is ebbing out, a hopeless case. They've left me here to die, like those slain on the battlefields from whom your mercies are removed. You have thrust me down to the darkest depths, your wrath lays heavy on me. Wave after wave engulfs me. You have made my friends to loath me, and they have gone away.

" 'I am in a trap with no way out. My eyes grow dim with weeping. Each day I beg your help. O Lord, I reach my pleading hand to you for mercy.

" 'Soon it will be too late. Of what use are your miracles when I'm in the grave? How can I praise you then? Do those in the grave declare your loving kindness and proclaim your faithlessness?

" 'Can the darkness speak to your miracles? Can anybody in the land of forgetfulness talk about your help? O Lord, I plead for my life and I will keep on pleading day by day. Oh, Jehovah, why have you thrown my life away? Why are you turning your face from me and looking the other way. From my youth I've been sickly and ready to die.

" 'I stand helpless . . . your fierce wrath has overwhelmed me. Your terrors have cut me off, they flow around me all the day long. Lover, friend, acquaintance, all are gone. There's only darkness everywhere.' "

Reverend Long paused and took a deep breath.

"There's a gloomy situation, isn't it?" he asked. "And yet the Psalmist raises the same question that we want to raise before God. Why? And yet we cannot say why.

"It's strange that in our inadequacy is where we come closest to God than ever before. We realize our own failings. We have no answers. We can only rejoice in what Gods does and says. We are called upon to make a faithful statement before others. The pain is great, the anguish is great.

"And yet through this whole experience we have to find a way to rise and praise God. That is why we are here. That is the purpose of this worship service: we come and praise God. For there is no other.

"As David worked through the pain and the heartache of the loss of his own son, as he wept and cried through the Eighty-eighth Psalm, the word comes. The moment arises where he goes, he washes his body, he anoints himself, he comes to worship. It's time to get on with the Lord's business.

"And it's at that moment in time, when David has worked through this whole situation with God, his faith has grown stronger, he's been tested beyond belief. At that moment in time, David can arise and cry out to God.

"Here, and only at this time can he say, 'Because the Lord is my shepherd, I have everything I need. He lets me rest in the meadow grass and leads me beside quiet streams. He restores my failing health, he helps me do what honors him the most. Even when walking through the dark valley of Death I will not be afraid. For You are close beside me, guiding all the way. You provide delicious food to me in the presence of my enemies. You have welcomed me as your guest, blessings overflow.

" 'Your goodness and unfailing kindness will be with me all my life and afterward I will live with you forever in your home.'

"The word of God for us today."

With Reverend Long's final words, the congregation stood for the hymn "All Hail the Power of Jesus' Name" and then one by one the mourners passed the casket and stepped into the sunshine. Six pall bearers, including Mitchell Sinclair, carried the tiny casket from the church.

A sobbing David was led out of the church by his Uncle Doug. His father, Charles David Smith, supported Becky.

"It's wrong, it's wrong," David kept saying through his tears. "No, no, no, no."

A long motorcade made the six-mile trip from Buffalo United Methodist Church west on Route 215 to the Bogansville United Methodist Church cemetery. As the cars moved slowly along the highway, they passed dozens of people standing at the sides of the road, crying. Some held signs reading "We love you." Children blew kissess. Adults bowed their heads in prayer.

The motorcade drew past the house where David grew up, past the home of his great-grandmother, where he and Susan had lived when they first got married and where they had brought Michael home from the hospital after he was born.

Next door to the house, a small church had placed a sign: "Our Prayers are with the Smith family."

At the cemetery, four tents stretched over the gravesite, shielding hundreds of flower arrangements from the sun. Rev. Long led the mourners in a final prayer, and then it was time to say goodbye. David was inconsolable. He bent his head over the casket, his heart breaking.

"I don't want to leave, I don't want to leave," he sobbed as he was led back to the car, clutching a photo of his sons.

As they left, David's father knelt in front of the casket. Through his tears, he looked at the next headstone, the grave of his son Danny.

"Once I had two sons and now I have one," he would say later. "Once I had two grandsons, and now I have none."

Charles David Smith bent and kissed the casket. "Bye, boys," he whispered.

[20]

In the days following the boys' funeral, the tabloid television shows jumped on the story. *A Current Affair* wrangled a coup: They paid Barbara Benson, David Smith's mother, for an exclusive interview they broadcast over five days. As part of the agreement, Barbara provided producers with a video from David and Susan's wedding, a diary Susan had kept shortly after the birth of Michael, and an anniversary card David had sent his wife a few months before they separated.

Crying quietly, Barbara Benson spoke of her son's shock at learning his estranged wife had killed their children.

"He kept saying he couldn't understand it," she said. "He has so many things he wants to talk to her about. Why did you kill them Susan? Why didn't you let me know that you were having difficulty, that you didn't want them anymore?"

She described her son today as a man consumed by grief. "He just paces a lot and looks at their pictures. He's trying to keep his mind busy and not constantly focus on this horrible event."

Barbara Benson said that David had been so hopeful that the carjacker would release the children unharmed. "We thought, the person who put Susan out of the car, well, there's an opportunity for a ransom," she said.

Her son, she added, was very protective of Susan in the days after the alleged carjacking. He worried about her, and treated her tenderly while authorities searched for their missing boys.

"He was so loving toward her the whole time," she said. "I don't mean in front of cameras—I mean all the time."

David, she said, had been angry that investigators kept calling and asking Susan to come in for questioning. "He was really resenting that law-enforcement agents were focusing on Susan when we felt that they should be out there looking for the children," she said.

Not for a minute, she said, did David even consider asking his wife if she had anything to do with the children's disappearance, even when some members of the press were speculating openly about her involvement. "He never asked," said Barbara Benson. "That would have been an insult. It was so absurd, so cruel. We thought it was all this media frenzy. He believed with all his heart."

Benson admitted she had had some reservations about her son marrying Susan at such a young age, but that she had held her tongue, figuring it wasn't her place to tell them what to do. After the couple separated, Barbara Benson said that David had decided on his own that the children were better off living with Susan, that she handled them better.

At the end of the interview, a tearful Barbara lamented, "I never thought that that marriage would result in something so horrible."

Susan's best friend, Donna Garner, also earned money for an interview. A producer from *Inside Edition* offered her $500 and eventually settled on $2,000. Donna did a short interview with the tabloid show.

David's sister, Becky, too, spoke on *Inside Edition*. She talked about her shock when she learned what her sister-in-law had confessed to doing.

"I just couldn't believe it," she said. "I was in total shock. I believed her. I had to hear it from David and my Dad before I really believed it."

As for Susan, Becky said, "She is one of the best mothers you'd ever meet. I don't hate her because this isn't Susan that did this. It was someone else, a different Susan."

Becky recalled that the day of the boys' funeral David had seen a news report quoting a *Newsweek* magazine article that said Michael had awakened as the car submerged in John D. Long Lake and that Susan had watched him struggle to get out of his carseat, something that officials insist is not true. David, she said, was nonetheless devastated by the report.

The day after Susan confessed, Oprah Winfrey, Phil Donahue, Sally Jessy Raphael, all set up shop in Union and ran shows dealing with how the town was handling the betrayal of Susan Smith and how the racial issue had threatened to divide the town.

Donahue and his staff broadcast from the gym at the University of South Carolina, and invited community leaders, ministers, and residents to speak out about the tragedy.

One woman, tears streaming down her face, angrily said that Susan Smith should pay for what she did. "I believe in my heart that she knew what she was doing when the car went down that ramp with those two poor little babies in the back seat."

"Vengeance is mine, saith the Lord," Donahue interrupted.

The woman grabbed the microphone back from Donahue. "I don't have to judge her," she shot back. "It's just a crying shame that two poor little lives are gone from this earth."

Rev. Bob Cato also spoke out on the program. He had been called at Fairview Baptist Church three times by one of Donahue's producers. Each time he had turned her down.

But the young woman wouldn't give up. "Reverend, we really want the perspective of a minister on the show," she told him the third time.

"You're going to persist, aren't you?" he asked.

She said she was. Cato came up with a solution. He would discuss it with Susan's mother and stepmother. He would let them decide. "I'm going over to the Russell family tonight," he told the producer. "I'm going to ask for permission to be on the show."

That night, Cato met with the Russells. Initially, they weren't sure it would be a good idea for him to appear on the *Donahue* program. But the pastor pointed out all the negative things people had been saying about Susan.

"Nobody's coming at it from a Christian perspective," he told them. "If I go on, I'll come at it from a Christian perspective, that there is forgiveness. I think the message needs to be received."

During the broadcast, Rev. Cato had an opportunity to speak briefly about forgiveness. A psychiatrist on the show also spoke in defense of Susan, suggesting to angry audience members that every individual has a breaking point.

Most of them, he pointed out, had not reached theirs.

After the show, Rev. Cato was deluged with calls and letters from *Donahue* viewers around the country. He was pleased that at least some people had heard his message of forgiveness.

One night, he received a phone call at almost midnight from a woman in Utah. She told him she had just seen him on *Donahue*, and apologized for the lateness of the hour. The show had aired earlier in Utah, and she hadn't factored in the time change.

But the woman had something she needed to say, something she had told no one before. She told the minister that she was a Christian and that not long ago, she gave birth to her first child, a son. She told the minister that she was horribly depressed after the baby's birth, and couldn't understand why. She told how she had painstakingly embroidered a pillow for his crib, and one night, as he was crying she had placed it over his face. The baby had begun to squirm beneath the pillow but the mother said she had continued to hold it in place.

Then, the mother told the minister, she had heard the doorbell. Her husband, she told him, was away on business and it was late, too late for a visitor.

It was a man who had accidentally rung the wrong doorbell. The woman directed him to the people he was planning to see, a neighbor's house down the block. The woman told the pastor that she believed that God had sent the man to save her baby's life, and to stop her from making a tragic mistake.

As she confessed her own story of nearing the edge, the woman said she was furious with a woman in the *Donahue* audience, who had proclaimed that Susan Smith deserved the electric chair. "I would love to pull the switch," the woman in the audience had said, as the *Donahue* crowd burst into applause.

"I'm more angry at that person than I am at Susan because I'm Susan," the woman told Cato.

The two talked for about half an hour. Before they hung up, the minister told her that he was glad she had called him and that she should seek out professional guidance.

"It's a troubling thing when you try to hold this in and keep this to yourself," he said. "Even though you shared this with me, I can't be there to counsel you. I would suggest you go to your pastor or a Christian therapist and tell them."

The woman promised she would.

Oprah Winfrey arranged an interview via satellite with Sara Singleton, David Smith's maternal grandmother. Although Susan might have endured a lot of hardships in her young life, Singleton said, nothing came close to excusing her murder of Michael and Alex. "A lot of us had things happen to ourselves in our childhood," the older woman said, "but most of us decided to accept responsibility for our actions."

Oprah also spoke to some of the town's angry residents and discussed how Susan's lie that she had been attacked by a black man had threatened to destroy Union's racial harmony. She closed with these words: "I believe that we all have to at some point come to terms with not being able to believe in the violence that can destroy us but believe in the power of God that can restore us."

Several of Susan and David's Toney Road neighbors appeared on *Sally Jessy Raphael.* Among them was Dot Frost. Tears streamed down Dot's face when Sally asked her about the pain of losing her own two sons.

Dot told Sally how Susan seemed to be such a good mother, how anyone, anyone on the block would have been happy to take in the children if she no longer wanted them.

Susan's childhood friend Stacey Hartley, who now has three small children of her own, also spoke on the show. "At first, I was in shock," she said. "I thought, 'There's no way.' Even if she said she did it, I don't believe it. This wasn't the Susan that I knew. The Susan I knew would never have done such a thing. It wouldn't have even crossed her mind."

When Sally Jessy Raphael addressed the racial issue, Gilliam Edwards, seated in the audience, jumped to his feet. He began to lash out so angrily, audience members yelled for him to sit down.

A renowned black minister, the Reverend A. J. Brackett, pastor of St. Paul Baptist Church in downtown Union for twenty years, insisted Edwards's tirade was unjustified. Union's black and white communities had forged stronger ties in the aftermath of Susan Smith's confession, he said. He pointed out that only a few black men had been stopped by investigators during their search for the alleged carjacker, and that only two had been brought to police headquarters for questioning.

After the show, Brackett received dozens of letters from blacks and whites nationwide, praising Union and its leaders for handling a potentially volatile situation so well.

Two weeks later, Reverend Brackett received a call from the wife of Bill Gibson, national executive board chairman of the National Association for the Advancement of Colored People.

"Jesse Jackson saw you on TV," Mrs. Lottie Gibson told him. "He knows what you did to try to keep down racial tension. He'd like to come in and help the healing process. He'd like to sit down with the city's leaders."

The minister, while pleased, said he needed to get back to her. He told her he was concerned about something Sally Jessy Raphael had said on her show: that the Reverend Jackson had called for a U.S. Justice Department investigation into the way the Union County Sheriff's Department had treated blacks during the investigation of the alleged carjacking.

Gibson told him that she believed Reverend Jackson had been misquoted. She promised to look into the matter and assured him that Reverend Jackson wanted to assist in forging ties between the races, not breaking them apart.

Brackett discussed Jackson's proposed visit to Union with Sheriff Wells and several other black ministers, including Allen Raines at First Baptist Church in Union. He then called Mrs. Gibson back and told her the city would be looking forward to the Reverend Jackson's visit.

The next day, Jesse Jackson, in South Carolina to give a speech in nearby Greenville, made the trip to Union. During a brief tour of town, he spoke to townspeople at St. Paul Baptist Church, the Union High School and John D. Long Lake.

At the church he met with about forty ministers and local leaders, including Union's mayor, Burt Williamson. Speaking from the lectern at St. Paul, Reverend Jackson talked about how rare it is to come across a town as racially united as Union. He told the group that he had not called for a Justice Department investigation of the sheriff's office, rather he had called the

Justice Department in the early days of the investigation and offered to make an appeal to the carjacker to turn himself in.

He told the Union leaders that walls were coming down between the races, and encouraged them to build bridges in their place.

Susan's brother, Scotty Vaughan, was already trying. The day after his sister confessed, he read a letter to the media:

On behalf of my family, we want to apologize to the black community of Union. It's really disturbing to us for thinking that anyone would think that this was ever a racial issue. I'm thankful for many of my black friends who called me and to comfort me and to say that they still love me.

It's a terrible misfortune that all of this happened, but had there been a white man, a purple man, a blue man on that corner that night, that would have been the description that Susan used. We apologize to all of the black citizens of Union and everywhere and hope you won't believe any of the rumors that this was ever a racial issue.

And I know that many of the people out there feel betrayed, just as my family and David's family feel betrayed. I want you all to know that me and my family and David's family, we really needed all that you've done, we needed all of your prayers and we still need your prayers.

If anyone earned high marks for calming a potentially volatile racial situation it was Sheriff Howard Wells. Union residents almost universally expressed their pride in the lawman, saying he represented their county well to the American people. Leaders of the black community praised him for his respectful, even-handed questioning of several black men in the early days of the investigation.

Even Gilliam Edwards was impressed. "That sheriff is cool," he said. "I have to give it to him. If it was someone else, some black person would have been dead."

Edwards called Wells "a fine man," who'd handled the difficult situation perfectly. "The way he did his duty, I'll shake his hand any day," he said. "I never thought I'd live in South Carolina and see a white sheriff treat black people in a fair and decent manner as that white sheriff did under the conditions. I never thought I'd live to see that—I thought I'd be dead and gone before someone would come along to be as decent as that sheriff was."

And while Edwards admits he's still angry that Susan Smith would name a black scapegoat for her crime, he says he doesn't hold investigators responsible for her words.

"You give credit where credit is due. I'm not going to say nothing just to say nothing. I'm going to say what I see and what I know and that's what I see and what I know."

In the weeks after the investigation, Wanda Wells beamed with pride as the praise being heaped on her husband and his handling of the Smith investigation. People frequently stopped her on the street and in the bank. They told her that her husband had made Union proud.

Still, Wanda wondered sometimes where the sheriff got his energy. During the nine-day investigation, she'd often drop off trays of deli food at his office but she doubted he was touching them. Once, she asked his secretary, Linda Jenkins, to make sure he ate.

Wanda recalled the look on Linda's face.

"Wanda, he don't listen to me," Linda had said.

Wanda had laughed. He didn't listen to her, either. Indeed, by the time Susan Smith confessed, Howard Wells had lost ten pounds. He'd slept only a few hours a night; some nights not at all.

A few weeks after Susan's arrest, Union held a Sheriff Wells Appreciation Day at the local armory. More than 100 friends and well-wishers stopped in to shake Wells's hand and thank him for a job well done. A sign greeted him with the words "Out of Tragedy, We Found Reason in Sheriff Howard Wells."

In fact, Wells has received more than a thousand letters from people across the nation praising his performance in the Smith case. Some came in to the sheriff's office; some were delivered to his home on Toney Road, to the faded yellow mailbox decorated with paintings of birds and the words "The Wells."

Sometimes, in the evenings, he and Wanda would read through the letters together. "I was only doing my job," he'd occasionally say, uncomfortable, as he looked up from an especially complimentary missive.

Even the President called to congratulate Wells, but the sheriff was too modest to immediately mention it, even to his wife. Wanda Wells heard the news from her niece, Brandy. The young woman had been visiting her mother in Union and stopped in to see her Uncle Howard. He had casually mentioned his conversation with the President.

That night, Wanda and Howard Wells watched the evening news in his office.

"Oh, by the way," Howard Wells said to his wife. "The President called."

"I heard," she said, smiling. "Brandy told me."

Her husband nodded. He went back to watching TV.

"Howard," Wanda said, impatiently. "What did he say?"

"He just thanked me for doing a good job and trying to calm the racial issue," her husband explained. "He said he was glad to see how everybody had worked together. It was a real nice conversation."

During the frantic days of the Susan Smith case, it became Wanda Wells's job to look in on Howard Wells's seventy-seven-year-old father, John, who lived just two blocks from his son's office in downtown Union.

Ordinarily it was Howard himself who visited his father daily, making sure he had whatever he needed. Although John Wells suffered from Lou Gehrig's disease, he was able to take care of himself well enough to live alone. It helped that he got a Meals on Wheels delivery every day for lunch. Still, it had been rough on him since his wife, Julia Mae, had died of cancer two years earlier, just after her son's election to sheriff.

John Wells didn't quite understand why his son wasn't able to see him during the two weeks of the Susan Smith case. Already he'd not seen his son for most of the summer, when Howard had gone to the FBI Academy in Quantico.

Wanda tried to explain to her father-in-law the importance of the case that had kept Howard away, but she wasn't convinced he understood. So one afternoon, when she took him to Spartanburg for a doctor's appointment, Wanda purposely drove by the courthouse to point out the crush of reporters.

"See all those trucks, all those satellite dishes?" she said. "Every time your son comes out this door, these cameras are in his face."

John Wells just stared.

"My goodness!" he exclaimed.

[21]

Following her arrest, Susan Smith was held without bail at the York County Jail. A three-minute hearing was held the next day before Judge Larry Patterson.

Inside, Solicitor Thomas Pope announced the charges. "State versus Susan Smith," he said. "Two counts of murder. The Court's aware that one of the potential penalties on murder is life and therefore she is entitled to a bond hearing before a general-sessions judge. It is my understanding that she has one, waived her right to be present, and two, that she is waiving her right to ask for a bond hearing."

Susan's attorney, David Bruck, said that she had. Bruck, a Columbia lawyer, specializes in death-penalty cases. He had been hired the night before by Susan's mother and stepfather. That morning, he'd met with Susan for just twenty minutes before the hearing.

The following day, Susan Smith was permitted to make a call from a pay phone. She called her mother, Linda Russell. The moment they heard one another's voices, mother and daughter cried.

Through her tears, Susan told her mother repeatedly how sorry she was, how she hadn't known what she was doing. She told her she missed her babies. "Nobody knew what was going on inside," Susan sobbed.

The jail, she told her mother, "was a living hell."

Before they said good-bye, Susan said, "I don't want you to hate me."

Linda Russell told her that no one in the family did.

David Smith saw his wife for the first time since she confessed to the murder of their children at a hearing on November 18. He was noticeably tense. He talked quietly to his father and to Margaret Frierson before it began.

Margaret had called David several days earlier to offer her support. Even though the mystery of what happened to the children had ended, the center would still be there for the family.

"Do you want us to come with you?" she'd asked.

"Do what you think you need to do," David had replied.

Margaret almost laughed. It was very like David not to ask a favor. She knew from her dealings with him in the past that he didn't like to put anyone out.

"David, do you want me to go or don't you?"

"Well," he said, "do you want to go?"

"I'd be happy to come. I would love to be there for you."

"Well, if you put it to me that way, yeah. Okay. Come."

The morning of the hearing, Susan entered the courthouse flanked by her attorney, David Bruck. She smiled quickly at her mother, but never met David's gaze. At the hearing before Circuit Judge John C. Hayes of Rock Hill, Solicitor Thomas Pope requested that Susan undergo a psychological examination by an impartial physician to determine Susan's criminal responsibility and competence to stand trial.

Susan's attorney firmly objected, saying an evaluation could later be used against Susan if the solicitor chose to seek a death penalty in the case. As the attorney talked about Susan's fragile mental state, Susan, her hair pulled back off her face with a barrette, removed her glasses and brushed away tears.

"Susan right now is a lot like a six-year-old child," Bruck said. "She cannot defend herself. She needs to be protected."

Pope was clearly exasperated.

"Mr. Bruck doesn't want us ever to have any neutral body to look at her," he argued to Hayes.

"This is the first time since I have been in office that I have seen this."

Hayes asked Pope to provide him with cases in which judges ordered psychiatric evaluations of defendants. The following week, Pope did, submitting a fifty-eight page brief. But ultimately, Hayes ruled against Pope. In a ruling in late November, Judge Hayes said that the request for a neutral examination was premature, especially since David Bruck has not yet said whether he will offer an insanity defense.

As for David, he was clearly shaken by seeing Susan in the courtroom. "David said he wanted to see her to see if he could understand any better," said his former high-school girlfriend, Kristy. "He said he wanted to talk to her. He saw her in the courtroom. There was a lot of hurt on him. He said it made it worse. He still doesn't understand."

Solicitor Thomas Pope has yet to announce whether he plans to seek the death penalty for Susan Smith. Under South Carolina law, it is permissible if the defendant is charged with the death of a child eleven years old or younger, or has killed more than one person by one act. The death penalty in the state is administered by lethal injection.

Pope has said that he will discuss his decision with David Smith. "I want to meet with the family at the appropriate time," he told reporters. "It's still too early."

Pope, in his two years as solicitor, had prosecuted three death penalty cases. In one case, the defendant pleaded guilty and received a sentence of life in prison, so did the second, when the jury was deadlocked on a sentence. The third one is on Death Row.

David had planned to speak to the press not long after he learned of the children's death, but at the last minute he tearfully told his father he could not do it.

Charles David Smith went in his place.

"I know you'd rather have him, but he's just not ready to face his public," David's father told the reporters, his voice breaking. "He's still torn up and he's still hurt. Speaking for David and myself and his stepmother Susan and Uncle Doug, who you have already met, I just want you to know that David loves each and every one of you. He's broken up. He want's his children back. That can't happen. All of you, may God bless all of you, okay?"

A few weeks later, David was ready. He spoke to Katie Couric on the NBC news show *Prime Time Live.* He said he agreed to the interview in order to thank all the people who sent their love, prayers and support. "Thanks for every single thing that you have done," he said.

David admitted that in the past month, he had received many offers to sell his story.

"It was never tempting," he said. "Yes, sure, I received lots of offers to go on these shows. They offered a lot of money to talk with them. I don't want to make one red cent off my two little boys, out of respect and dignity for them."

He talked about the night that he got the call about the alleged carjacking. Susan, he said, was hysterical. "I had to literally pick her up," he said.

Couric asked him what kind of mother Susan had been to Michael and Alex. "She was great, she really was," David said. "She was a very dedicated, devoted mother to those two children. They were her heart, just like they were mine. They were her life, just like they were mine."

He smiled as he showed Couric a photo of the two boys playing inside a clothes basket. "You don't know how much they enjoyed a simple clothes basket," he said. "How they would play in that clothes basket for hours. A simple clothes basket."

Michael, he added, "loved to do what his daddy was doing."

He told Couric that throughout the days the boys were missing, he had believed the children would return safely.

"I always believed that they were okay," he said. "I had that assurance in myself that they were okay. Out there somewhere, I didn't know where, but they were being taken care of adequately." The futile search, he said, was devastating. "It would tear me back down emotionally," he said. "Any little hope you have inside was dropped back down to zero."

And David said that he never doubted that Susan was telling the truth. "I believed her one hundred percent," he said. He talked about the polygraph test, and how Susan had told him she may have failed. "She wasn't sure if she failed," he said. "She believed from what they told her that she did fail it. She thought that the local law enforcement were starting to doubt her. But I never did. Not for a fleeting instant."

When Katie Couric asked him his reaction to Susan's confession, his words came haltingly. "I was heartbroken," he said carefully. "I felt empty. I felt hollow. I felt betrayed. Everything was running together."

David said that he wanted to see Susan. "I've got certain questions that I need answers to before I have my own peace of mind," he said.

But the young man refused to elaborate when Couric asked him what, in fact, he would ask her if he could. His questions, he explained, were personal.

He talked about going to see the lake. "It was something I felt I had to see," he said. "I just had to take a look."

David says that every day he thinks back to the last time he saw his sons. "It's good to be able to look back on that and be able to smile," he says. "I miss those little smiles that they can give. They would take this whole earth and turn it upside down."

22

Even today, visitors crowd the shores of John D. Long Lake and pay their respects to the Smith boys at the Bogansville cemetery. Thousands have brought flowers and balloons emblazoned with the words "We Miss You," and "We Love You." They leave poems and letters by the boat ramp, and along the edge of the water. At the cemetery, children leave toys and stuffed animals in memory of the murdered boys.

One letter, signed by Carol A. Sullivan, is mounted by the grave, a picture of the children framed at the top.

It reads:

The whole nation looked for you. We searched and hoped and prayed. But nothing could have prepared us for what we found out that day. We will never understand this. We keep asking and asking why.

We wanted so much to find you. We can't simply say good-bye.

It hurts us all so deeply. Millions of tears we've cried. If our love and tears could have spared you, you never would have died.

The nation fell in love with you. In death we love you still. It may take us forever for our broken hearts to heal.

Two precious hearts stopped beating. Four beautiful eyes are at rest. Jesus has you with him now and we know you're with the best.

It broke our heart to lose you but you did not go alone. A part of us went with you, when Jesus took you home.

Another, left by eleven-year-old Cyndi Waters from Taylors, South Carolina, was written on two torn memo pages. In it she wrote:

Michael and Alex. You ment [*sic*] a lot to people in this world. You brought us this close. People from everywhere came down to the Lake. You ment a lot. I do not see how your mother could do this. You ment a lot to this world. It sent a message to the people of your town. Everyone prayed for you to return home safe. Your mother lied but she still may love you. Your dad loved you.

Listenership has soared for Carlisle Henderson's daily *Gospel Hour.* In the early days of the

Smith story, he talked about forgiveness almost every day. He had cringed at some of the bitter words he'd been hearing around town.

"Drag her down Main Street," one woman suggested.

"Put her in the backseat of the car and drown her, like she did to those kids," said another.

On the air, Carlisle begged his listeners to show restraint.

"Please, please, be careful what you say," he told them. "Vengeance is mine, saith the Lord. It could be your daughter, your sister. It could be your mother. God will do the judging. We are not to judge. It could have happened in my family, my wife's family, my son's family. Love this family less? I love this family more today then I ever did."

For the past eight years, ever since he began his show, Carlisle ended the hour by saying, "God loves you, and so do I." After Susan's arrest he began saying, "God loves you, Susan, and so do I."

In time, he began to get calls from listeners agreeing with him, saying people needed to pray for Susan Smith. Carlisle told his listeners that he did not know why this tragedy happened in Union but perhaps God had a plan.

"This town needed revival," he said. "We've taken each other for granted, we're not visiting our neighbors, everyone's in such a hurry. God may be saying, 'Wake up, Union.' God could be trying to tell us something."

Not long after Susan's confession, Carlisle's wife, Georgia, called Linda Russell.

"Linda, this is Georgia Henderson," she said warmly. "I just called to tell you we love you and if we can do anything, we're here. And we're praying for you."

"I appreciate that," Linda Russell said, her voice weary, "but please pray for Susan."

"We already are."

During the weekend of the funeral, Shirley and Rick McCloud escaped. They spent two days with friends in Myrtle Beach, strolling on the beach and staying up late, talking. The next Monday morning they woke early and left the house just after 6:30, driving the short distance down the winding road to John D. Long Lake.

It was something, they had decided, they needed to see.

But to their surprise, they were not alone, despite the early hour. A photographer for the *Spartanburg Herald* was already at work, trying to capture a mood shot of the sun rising over the water.

Shirley's face fell when she saw him. "Please don't take my picture," she told him, as she and Rick began to walk down the boat ramp. "We thought we'd come early enough where no one would be here. Please don't ask us anything."

He didn't.

In the days since, things have quieted down, but not completely. Passersby take snapshots of the McCloud house and ring the doorbell, wanting to meet them. A few weeks after the confession, a woman showed up saying she'd locked her keys in her car and needed to use the phone.

"Now, you're Shirley McCloud?" she'd asked.

Shirley did not mince words. "Do you want to use my phone, or are you here to get a good look at me?" she wanted to know. "I'll give you a phone and you can call whoever you want, but please hurry up and get off my porch."

She does not go down to the lake anymore. She used to, sometimes in the evening, on a walk with her husband. There is nothing there, Shirley believes that she wants to see.

Dot Frost sees Susan and David Smith's darkened house every night from her living room window. She does not understand, she never will.

"She could have asked the Lord to help her," she often thinks. "He's helped us."

When she learned that Susan had told investigators she wanted badly to commit suicide, Dot felt no sympathy. *If she's going to take a life, she should have taken her own,* she thought. *I would take my life before those boys.*

But she believes that Susan will live to regret

her decision every moment of her life. "Lord's going to pay her back," Dot often reminds herself. "She won't never get over those two little boys. He'll punish her for what she did. I think about mine everyday.'

Now and then, she thinks about what might have been. "She could have left those young-uns on my porch," she'll say. "We don't have money, but we would have taken 'em. They was darling."

In the weeks since the funeral, David Smith has not returned to work at Winn-Dixie, although the supermarket continues to pay him his full salary. He stopped into the store the day after the burial, however, to thank his friends and co-workers for all of their support. Later that week, he visited the lake. He told his family it was something he needed to see.

The postal service reported that it received more than 20,000 letters, cards, and packages for David; about half of them are in boxes in his Lakeview Road apartment. Susan Smith received about 100 letters, which have been forwarded to where she is incarcerated. There, her lawyer screens them.

David's father and stepmother remained in Union for many weeks after the funeral for the children. The young man's relationship with his mother, which had been rocky, was further strained after her appearance on *A Current Affair.*

On November 22, two weeks after the funeral, David filed a countersuit in his divorce from Susan. In it he asks for a divorce on the grounds of adultery. He has also asked for the return of the Mazda.

In the counterclaim, his lawyer stated, "The minor children are now deceased due to very tragic circumstances. The issues of custody, visitation, and child support are therefore moot . . . the children of the Plaintiff and Defendant were tragically killed in this automobile and the Plaintiff believes that he should be entitled to exclusive title, control, and possession of this automobile so that he can see that the same is properly disposed of."

Susan has been transferred to the Women's Correctional Facility in Columbia, 70 miles from Union. She was given a physical and psychological evaluation and put on a twenty-four-hour suicide watch. A guard checks on her every fifteen minutes. In a six-by-fourteen-foot cell, she keeps a Bible, a blanket, and her glasses. She wears a paper gown.

Her attorney has yet to announce whether he will offer an insanity defense. If he does, it is strongly believed that he will bring up the sexual abuse charges Susan claimed against her stepfather.

Retired Judge David Wilburn, who sealed the court documents, has announced that he may consider unsealing the records. Not long after stories of the alleged molestation appeared in the press, Susan's brother, Scotty told *The State* newspaper in Columbia that he had not heard anything about the abuse charges until the day his sister was arrested. He said the family loves Bev Russell. "He has been the foundation for all of us," Scotty said. "If it did happen, it was very out of character for him. I'm sure it was a mistake."

In the days since the stunning confession, Susan Smith's cousin Mary Hickson sums up much of how the people who loved the young woman feel about her today.

"As much as I knew Susan," Mary said, "I still do not understand what happened. I think something drastic changed that night in a matter of seconds. In no way do I believe that she had intentions to do anything to those children. I think maybe she was sitting there thinking, trying to figure out all her problems, and just lost it. And in the end she just panicked and didn't know what to do."

And so, too, the neighbor who saw Susan and the children just a few days before the murder will not forget the image emblazoned forever in her mind, the resonance of the words she last heard from a young woman now standing accused of the ultimate crime. Susan, the woman said, had been cooking black-eyed peas and cornbread. She had Alex in her arms and the child began to fuss, squirming to get free. Susan told him, "Now, Alex, I'm going to have to put you down because you're going to get burned and I won't want to hurt you."

They were prophetic words, indeed. Now, the light blue plastic kiddie pool in the carport of David and Susan Smith's Toney Road home is left crumbled and half filled with water, collected from the day's rain. A bird feeder hangs empty on the tree in the front yard.

And in the streets of Union, across the nation and throughout the world, the question remains unanswered, the enigma that is Susan Leigh Vaughan Smith remains.

It is she alone who must face the stark truth of what she did that night in the hazy blackness of John D. Long Lake. And though she has said what happened that night was a mistake, a horrible mistake that she instantly yearned to take back, it was the act that ended the trust of a mother's heart, of a love meant to flow unparalleled and unchallenged. It is one that not only she must live with, but one that remains forever etched in the souls of those who were touched by Michael and Alex Smith.